MYTHOLOGY GRAPHICS

THESEUS AND THE MINOTAUR

A MODERN GRAPHIC GREEK MYTH

BY JESSICA GUNDERSON

ILLUSTRATED BY LE NHAT VU

CAPSTONE PRESS
a capstone imprint

Published by Capstone Press, an imprint of Capstone
1710 Roe Crest Drive, North Mankato, Minnesota 56003
capstonepub.com

Library of Congress Cataloging-in-Publication Data is available
on the Library of Congress website.

ISBN: 9781669059066 (hardcover)
ISBN: 9781669059318 (paperback)
ISBN: 9781669059325 (ebook PDF)

Summary: Theseus is bold. He's brave. And he's about to go head-to-head
with a mythological monster. Yikes! But Theseus has no fear. He goes into
the labyrinth to face the Minotaur—a monster that's half-man, half-bull—
with only a magical ball of yarn to guide him. Find out if Theseus makes it
out of the maze alive in this modern, graphic retelling of a classic Greek myth.

Editorial Credits
Editor: Alison Deering; Designer: Jaime Willems; Production Specialist:
Whitney Schaefer

Printed and bound in the USA. PO 5626

TABLE OF CONTENTS

CHAPTER 1

WHAT'S UNDER THE ROCK?

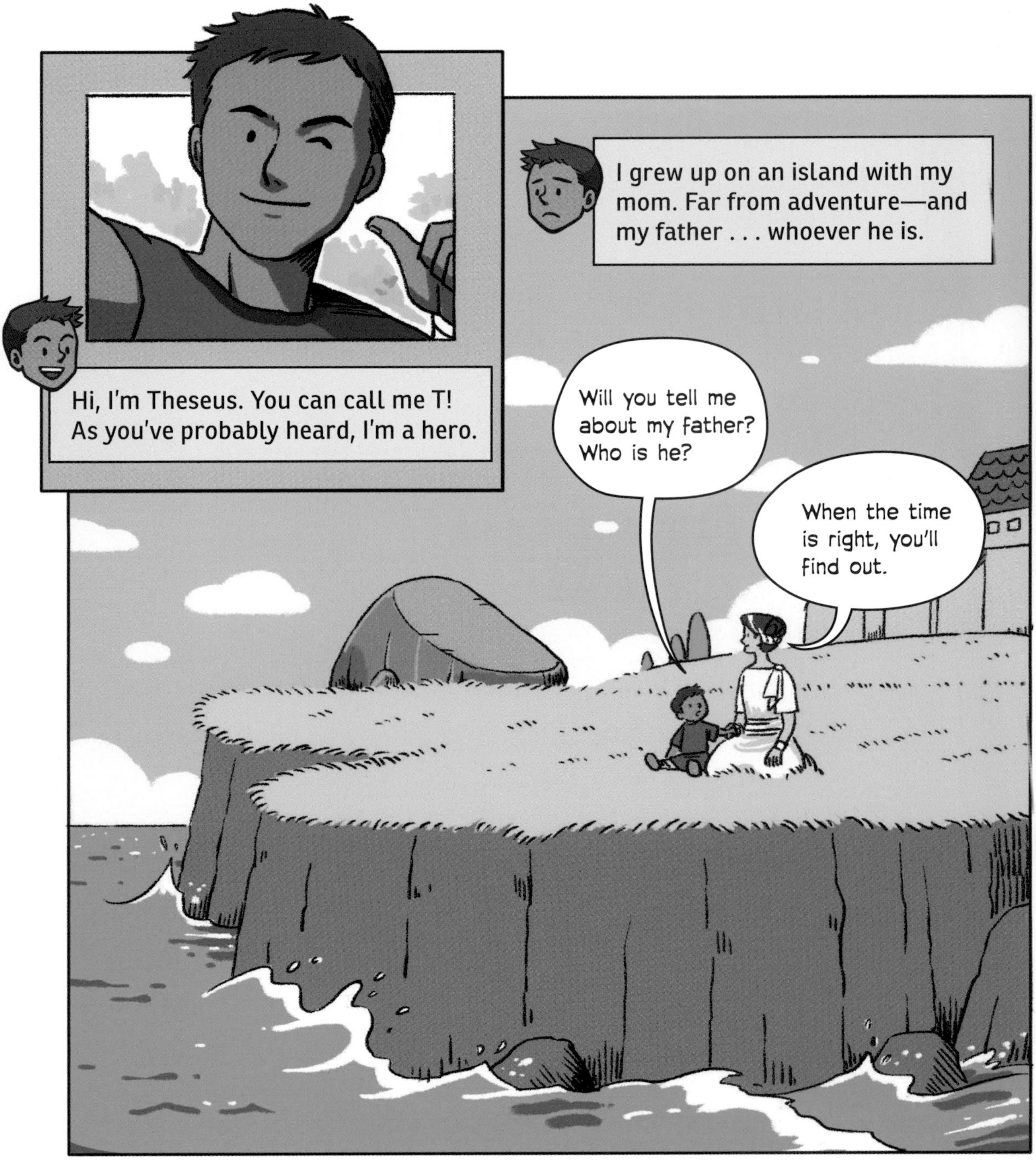
Hi, I'm Theseus. You can call me T! As you've probably heard, I'm a hero.
I grew up on an island with my mom. Far from adventure—and my father . . . whoever he is.
Will you tell me about my father? Who is he?
When the time is right, you'll find out.

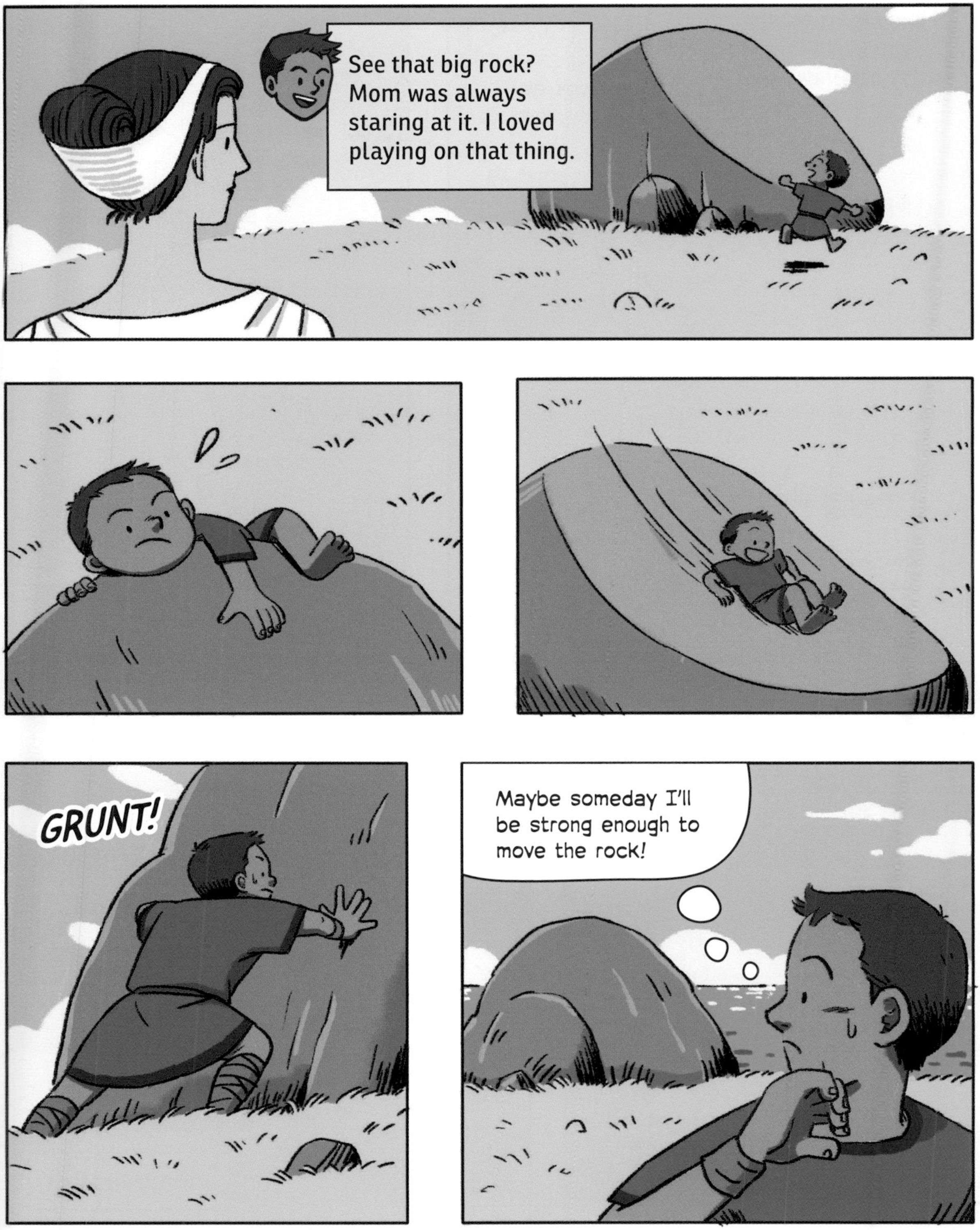
See that big rock? Mom was always staring at it. I loved playing on that thing.
GRUNT!
Maybe someday I'll be strong enough to move the rock!

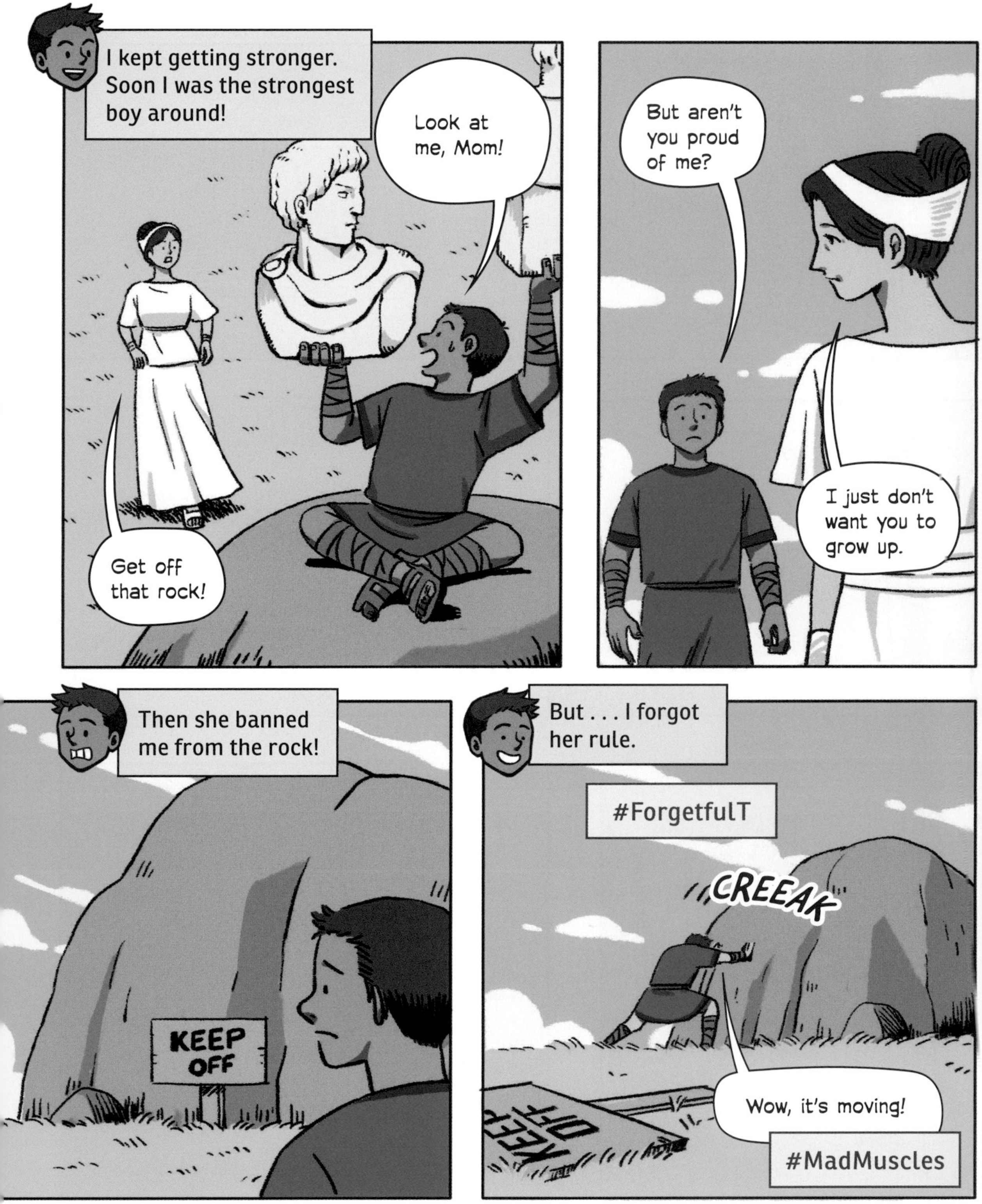
I kept getting stronger. Soon I was the strongest boy around!
Look at me, Mom!
Get off that rock!
But aren't you proud of me?
I just don't want you to grow up.
Then she banned me from the rock!
KEEP OFF
But . . . I forgot her rule.
#ForgetfulT
CREEAK
Wow, it's moving!
#MadMuscles

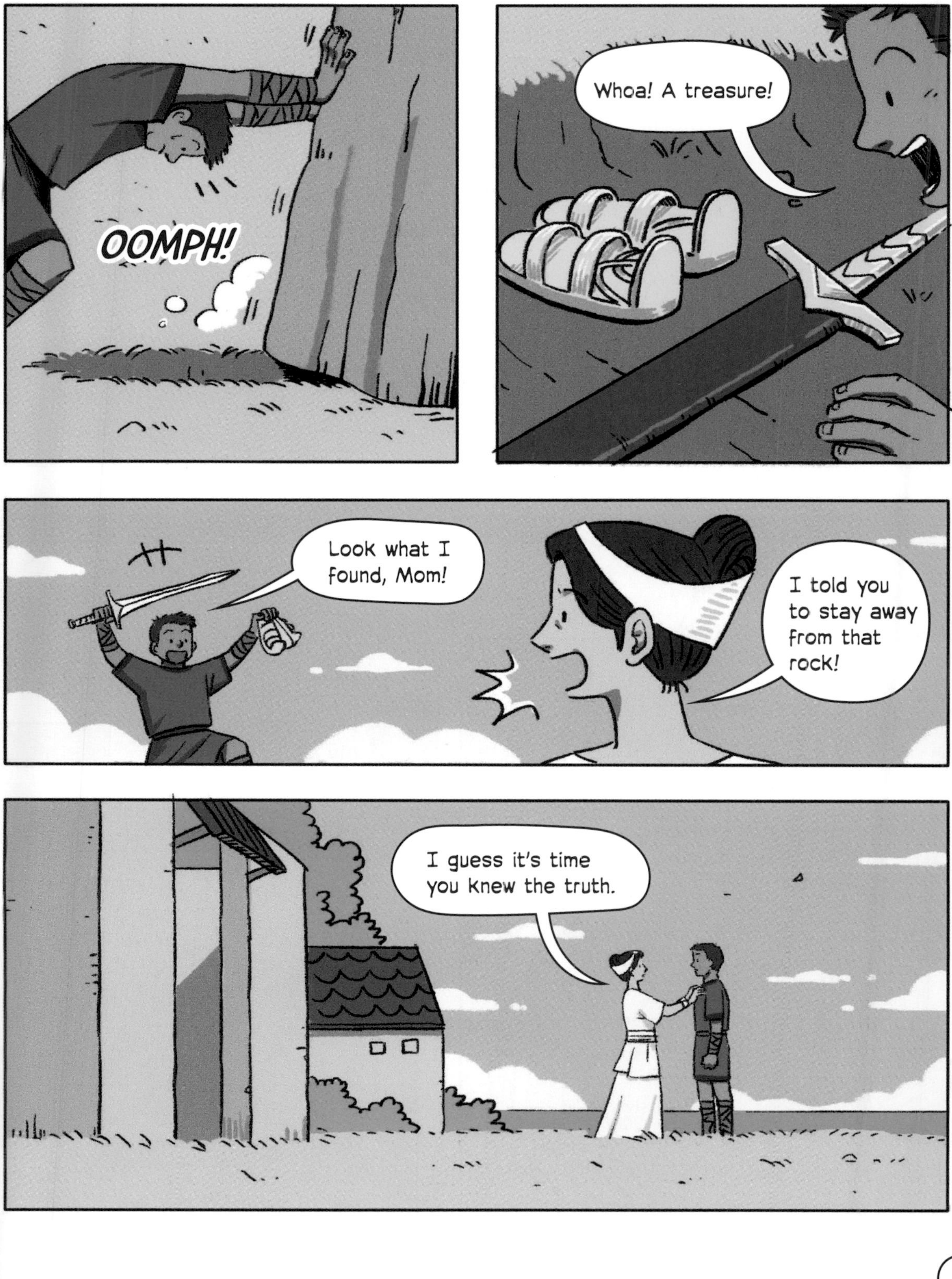
OOMPH!
Whoa! A treasure!
Look what I found, Mom!
I told you to stay away from that rock!
I guess it's time you knew the truth.

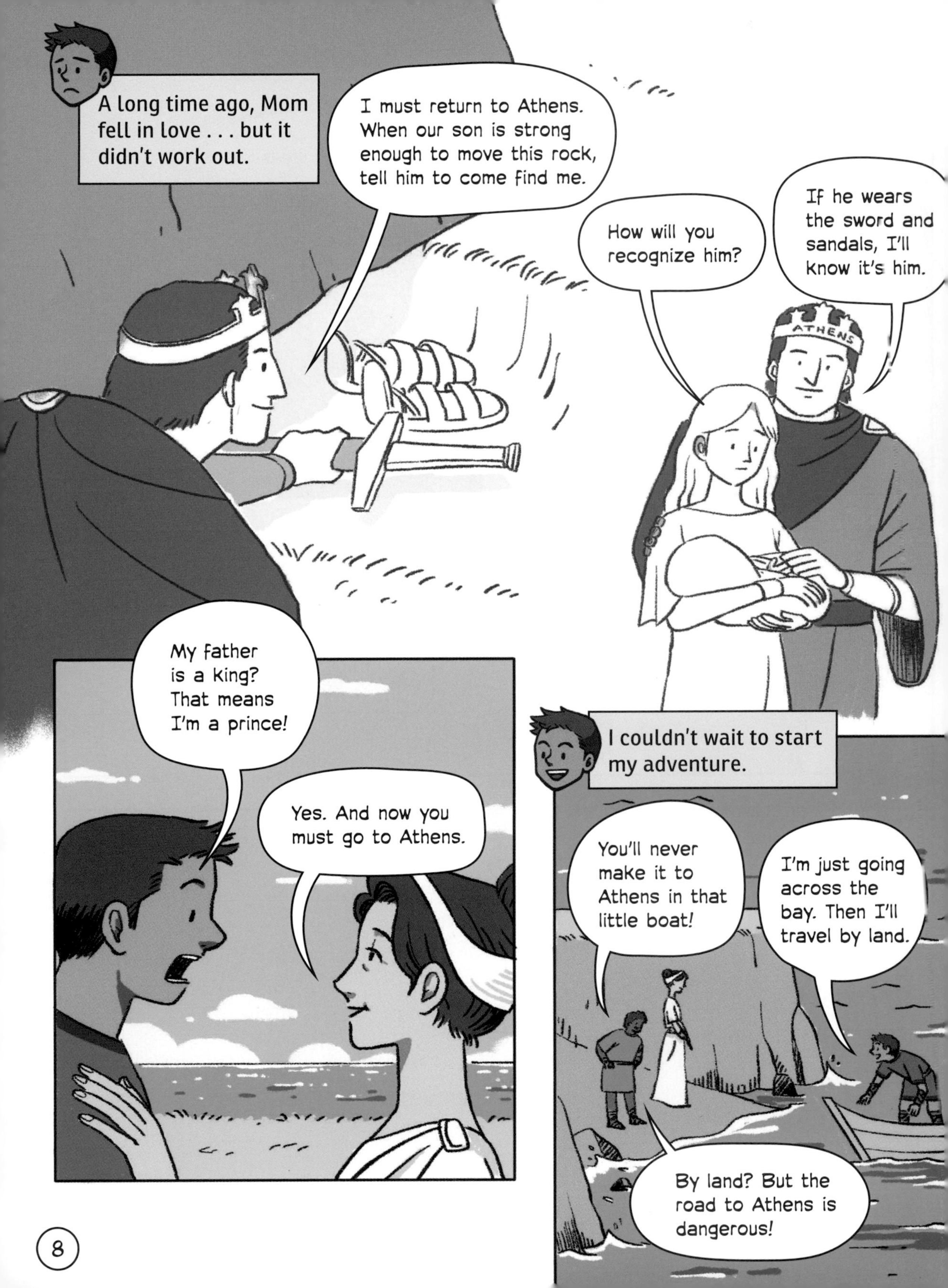
A long time ago, Mom fell in love . . . but it didn't work out.
I must return to Athens. When our son is strong enough to move this rock, tell him to come find me.
How will you recognize him?
If he wears the sword and sandals, I'll know it's him.
ATHENS
My father is a king? That means I'm a prince!
Yes. And now you must go to Athens.
I couldn't wait to start my adventure.
You'll never make it to Athens in that little boat!
I'm just going across the bay. Then I'll travel by land.
By land? But the road to Athens is dangerous!

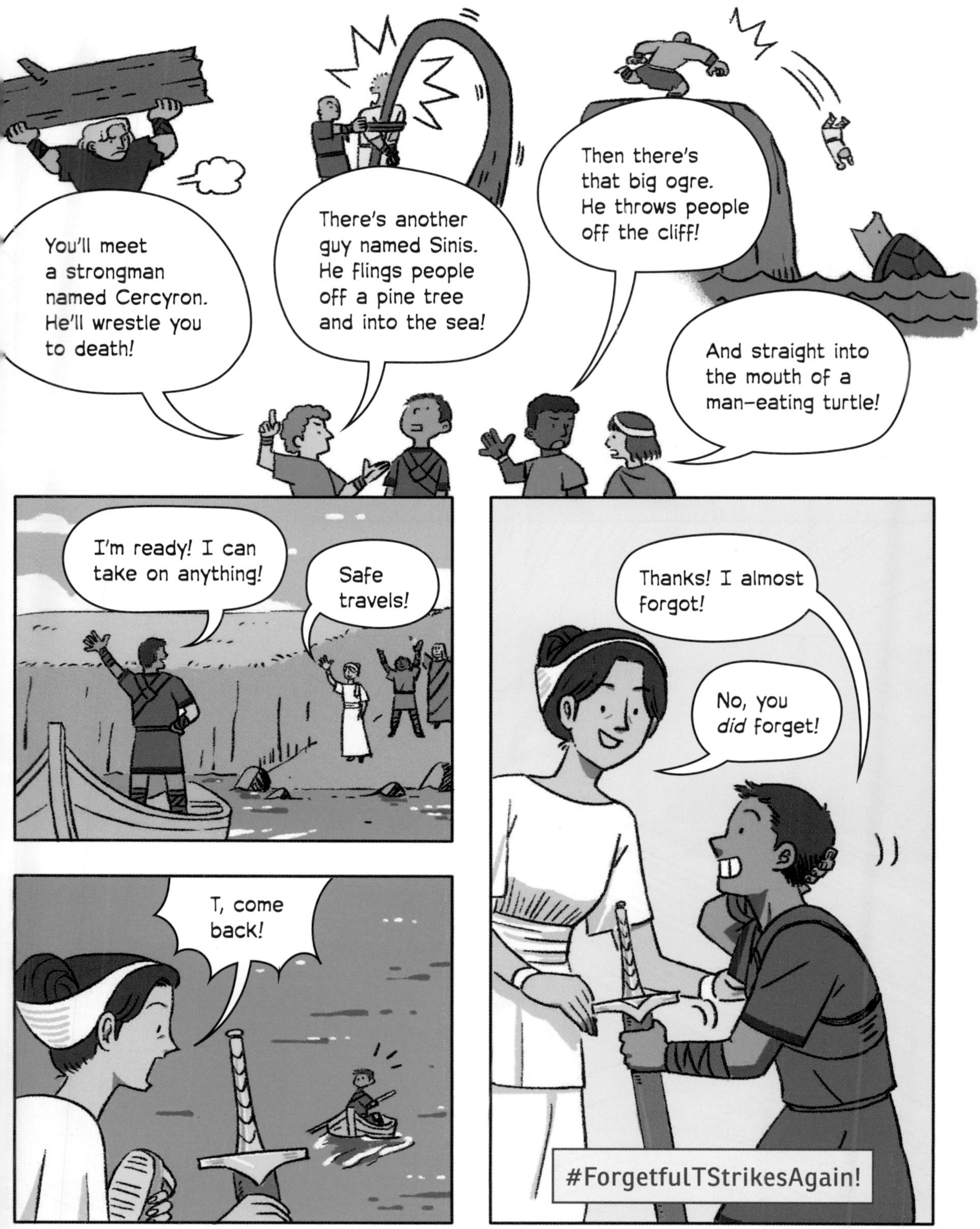
You'll meet a strongman named Cercyron. He'll wrestle you to death!
There's another guy named Sinis. He flings people off a pine tree and into the sea!
Then there's that big ogre. He throws people off the cliff!
And straight into the mouth of a man-eating turtle!
I'm ready! I can take on anything!
Safe travels!
T, come back!
Thanks! I almost forgot!
No, you *did* forget!
#ForgetfulTStrikesAgain!

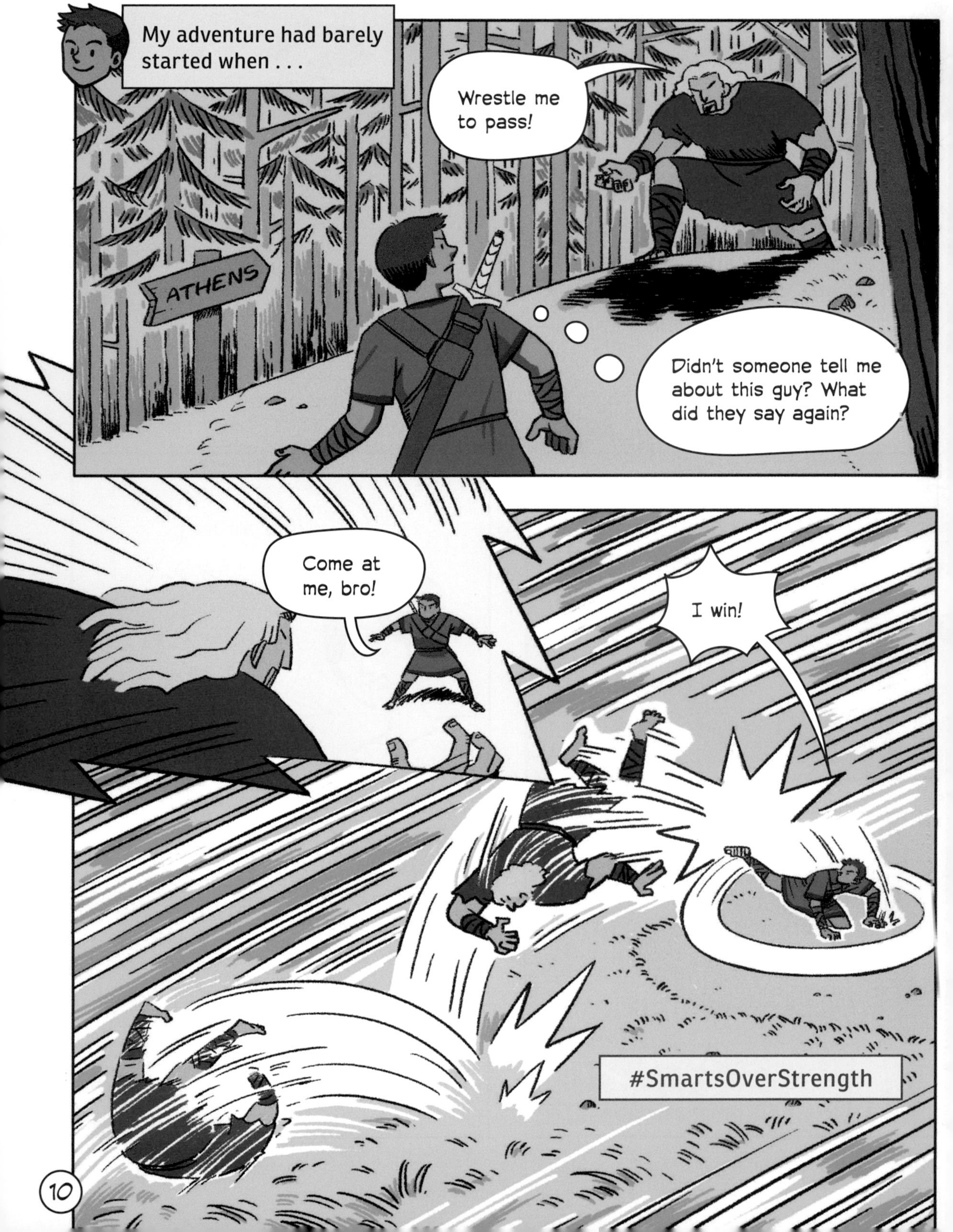

My adventure had barely started when . . .
Wrestle me to pass!
ATHENS
Didn't someone tell me about this guy? What did they say again?
Come at me, bro!
I win!
#SmartsOverStrength

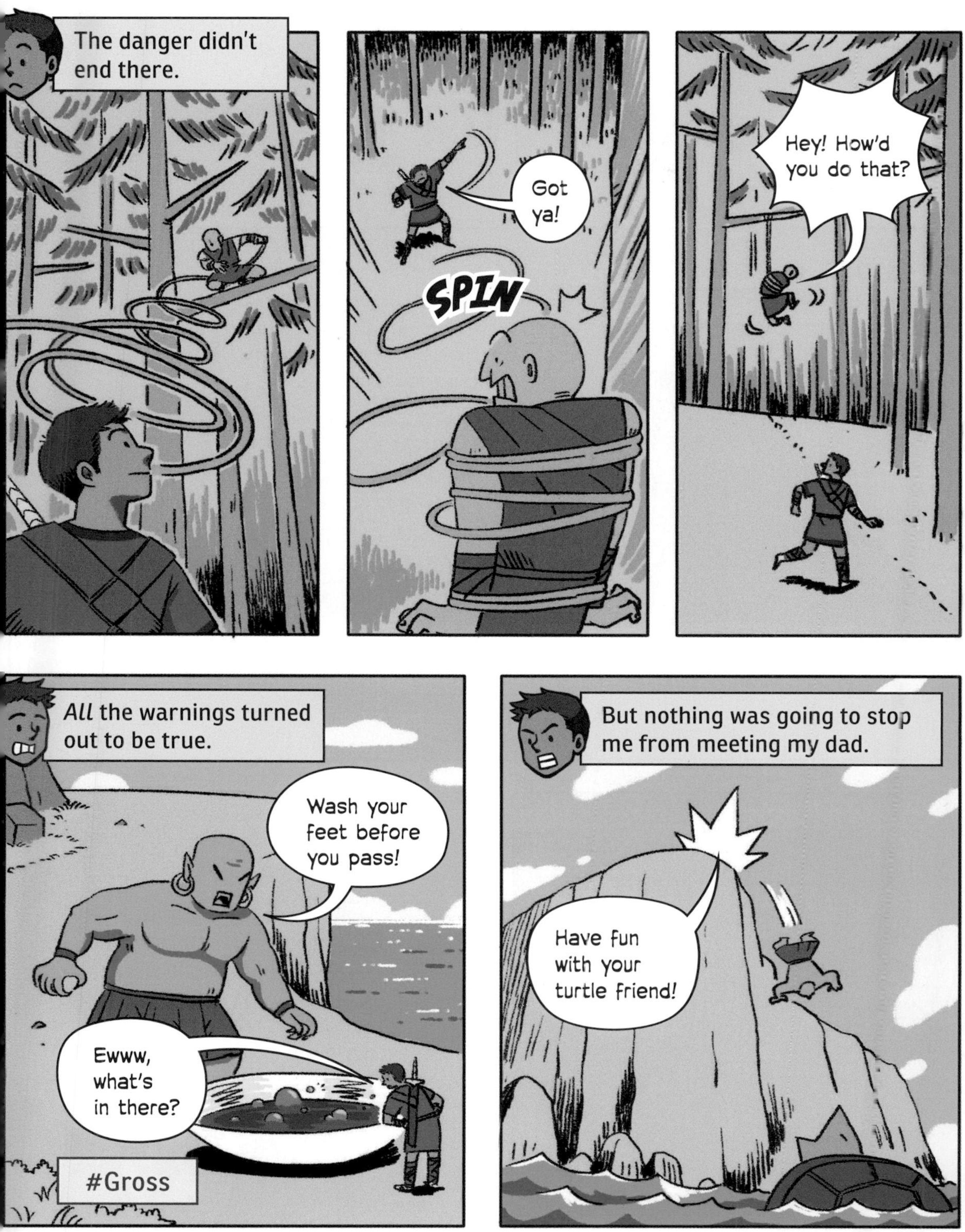
The danger didn't end there.
Got ya!
SPIN
Hey! How'd you do that?
All the warnings turned out to be true.
Wash your feet before you pass!
Ewww, what's in there?
#Gross
But nothing was going to stop me from meeting my dad.
Have fun with your turtle friend!

CHAPTER 2

PRINCE FOR A DAY

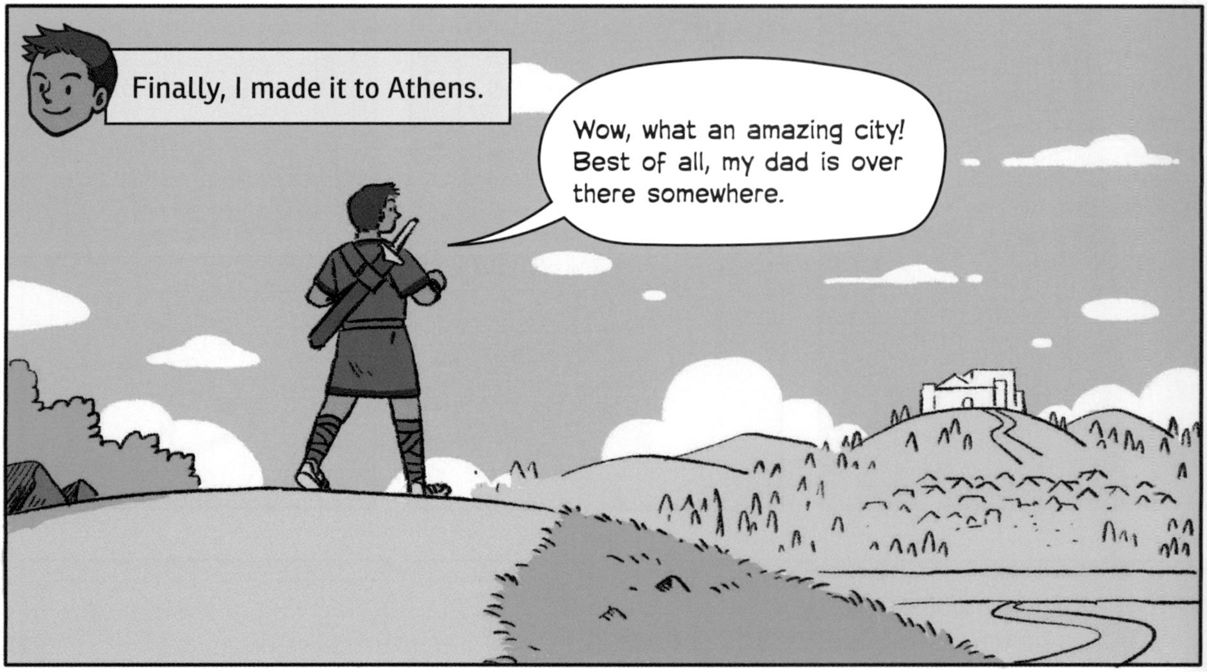
Finally, I made it to Athens.
Wow, what an amazing city! Best of all, my dad is over there somewhere.

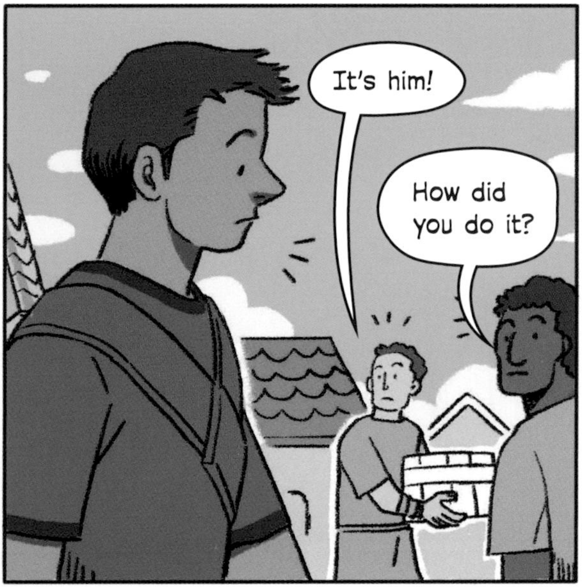
It's him!
How did you do it?

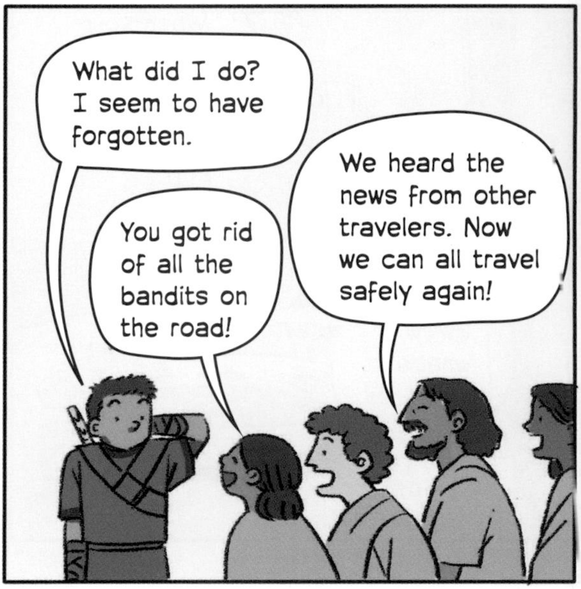
What did I do? I seem to have forgotten.
You got rid of all the bandits on the road!
We heard the news from other travelers. Now we can all travel safely again!

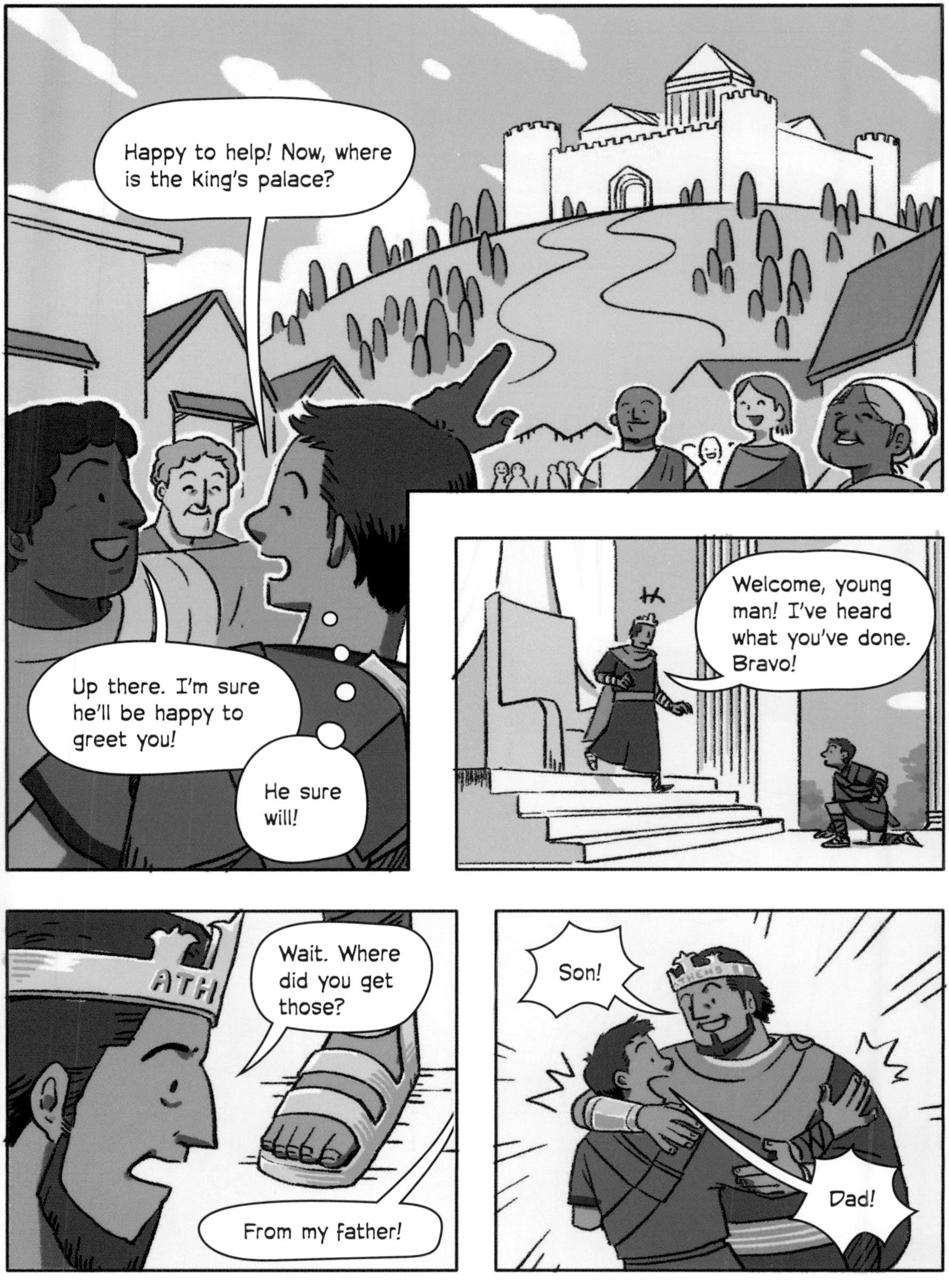
Happy to help! Now, where is the king's palace?
Up there. I'm sure he'll be happy to greet you!
He sure will!
Welcome, young man! I've heard what you've done. Bravo!
ATH
Wait. Where did you get those?
From my father!
Son!
Dad!

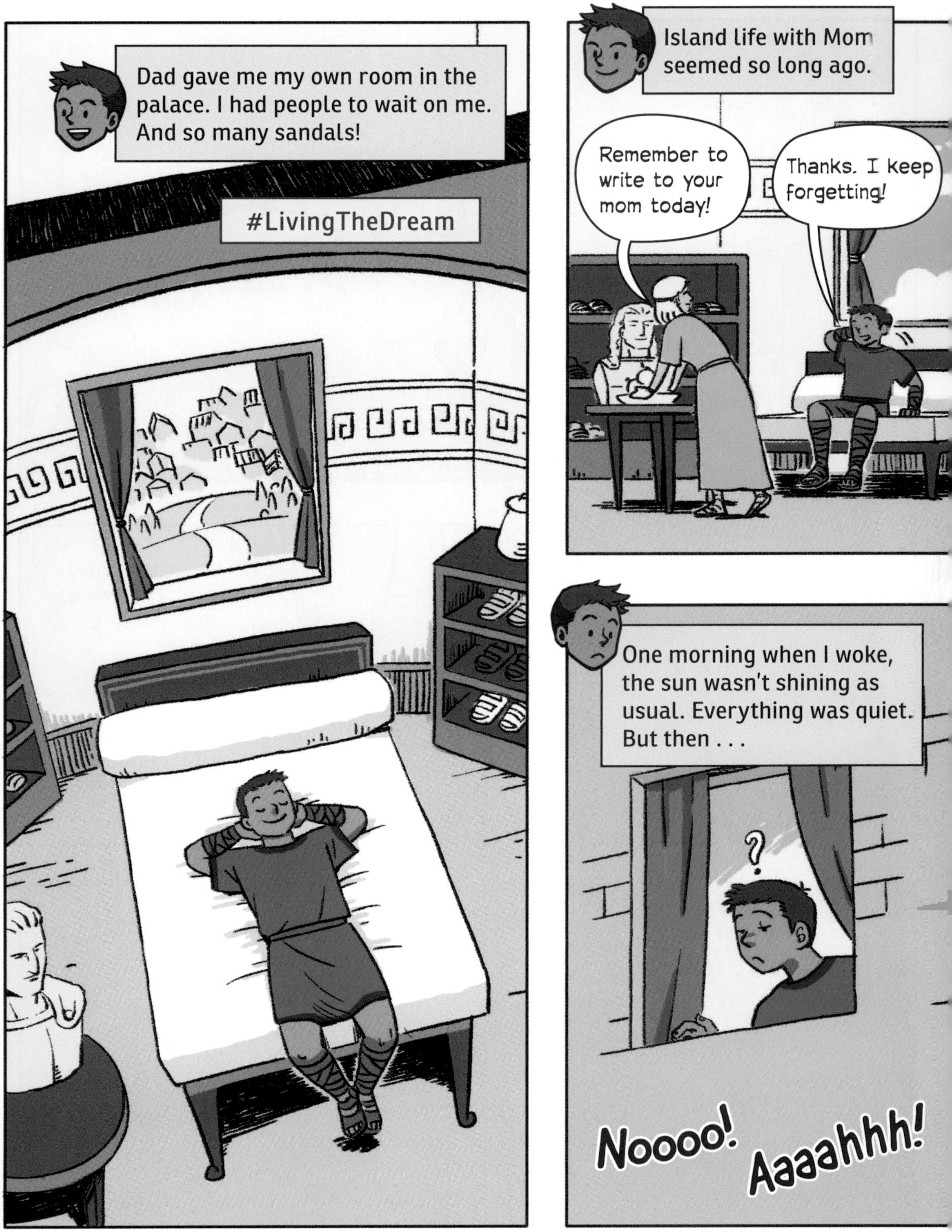
Dad gave me my own room in the palace. I had people to wait on me. And so many sandals!
#LivingTheDream
Island life with Mom seemed so long ago.
Remember to write to your mom today!
Thanks. I keep forgetting!
One morning when I woke, the sun wasn't shining as usual. Everything was quiet. But then . . .
Noooo!
Aaaahhh!

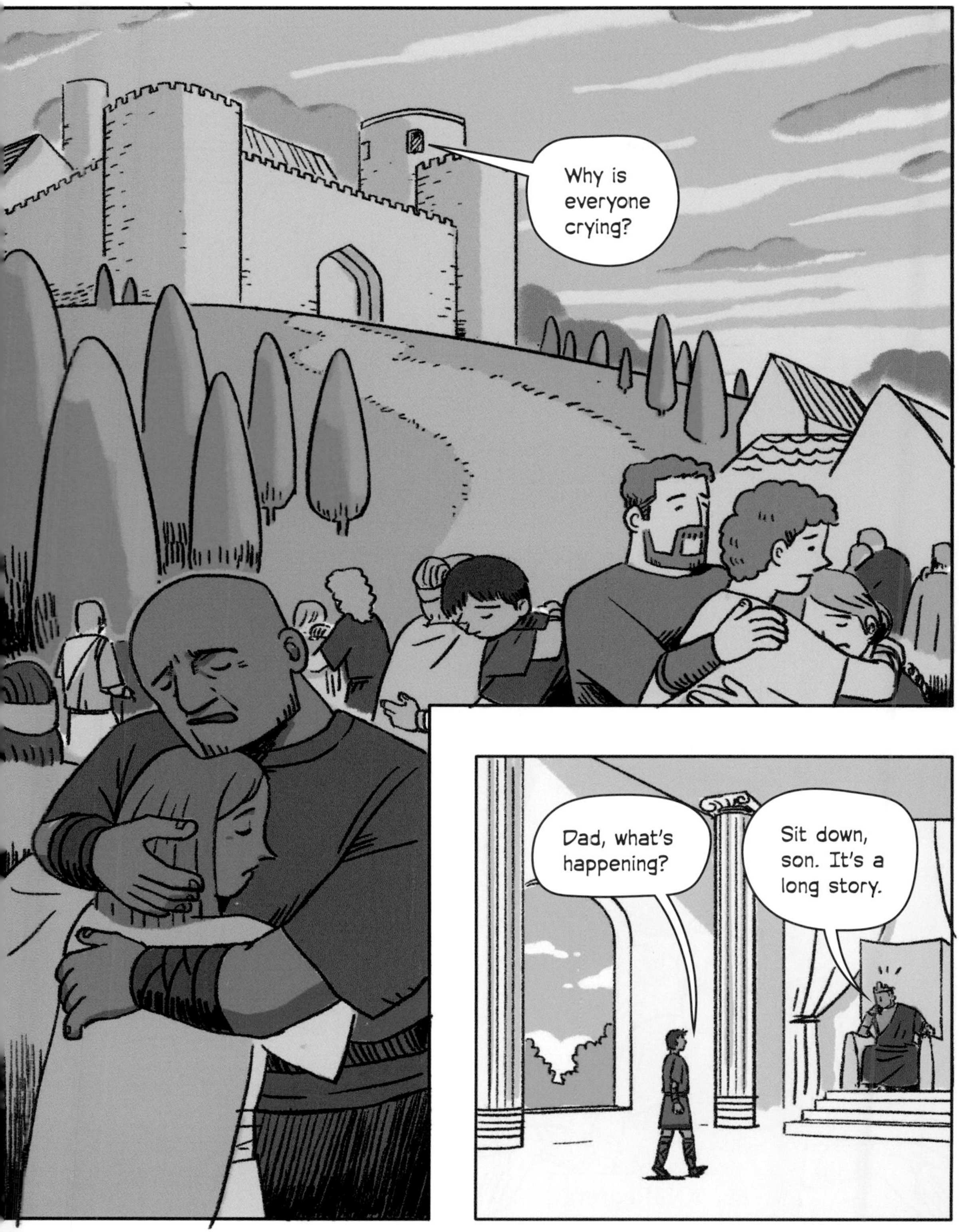
Why is everyone crying?
Dad, what's happening?
Sit down, son. It's a long story.

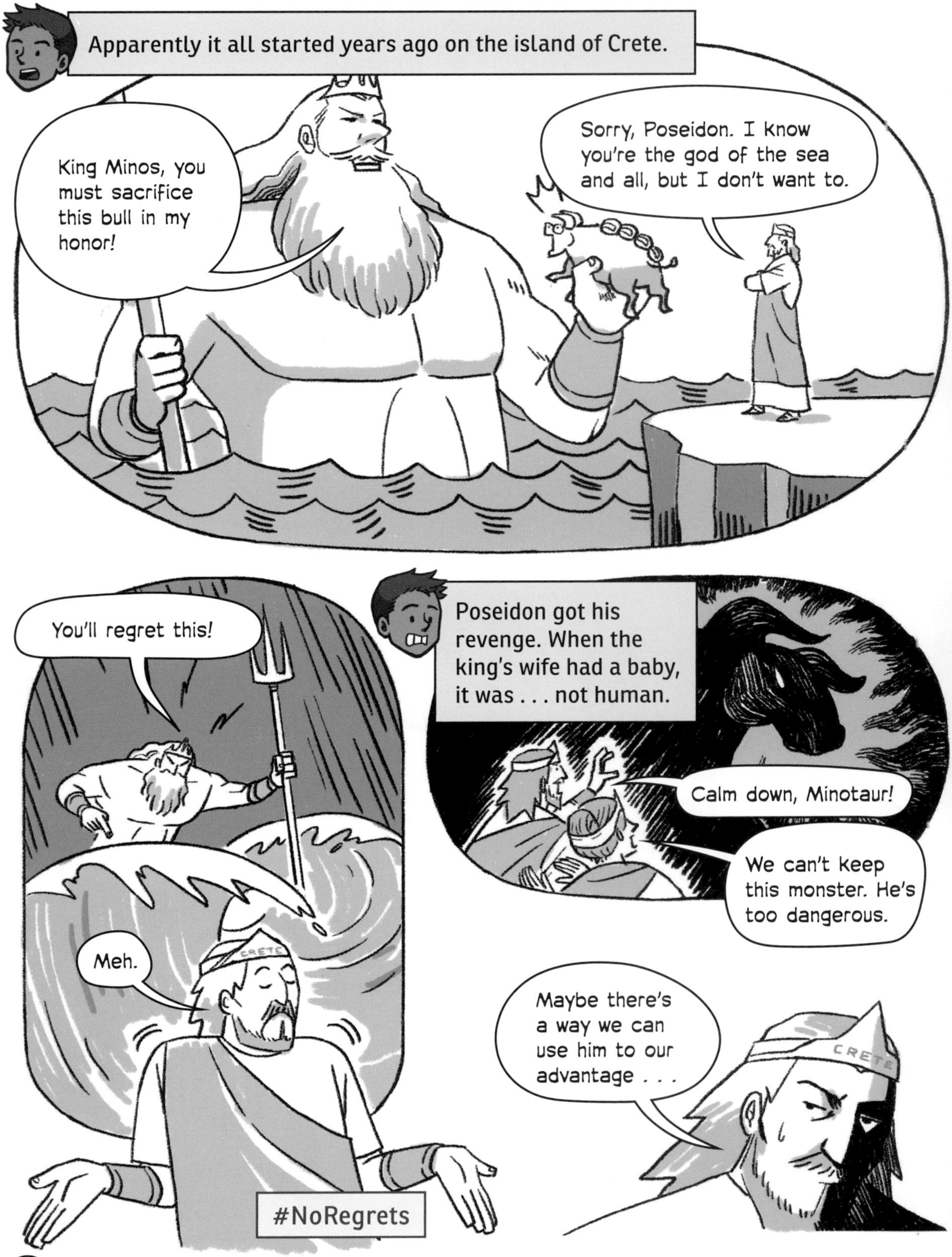
Apparently it all started years ago on the island of Crete.
King Minos, you must sacrifice this bull in my honor!
Sorry, Poseidon. I know you're the god of the sea and all, but I don't want to.
You'll regret this!
Meh.
#NoRegrets
Poseidon got his revenge. When the king's wife had a baby, it was . . . not human.
Calm down, Minotaur!
We can't keep this monster. He's too dangerous.
Maybe there's a way we can use him to our advantage . . .
CRETE

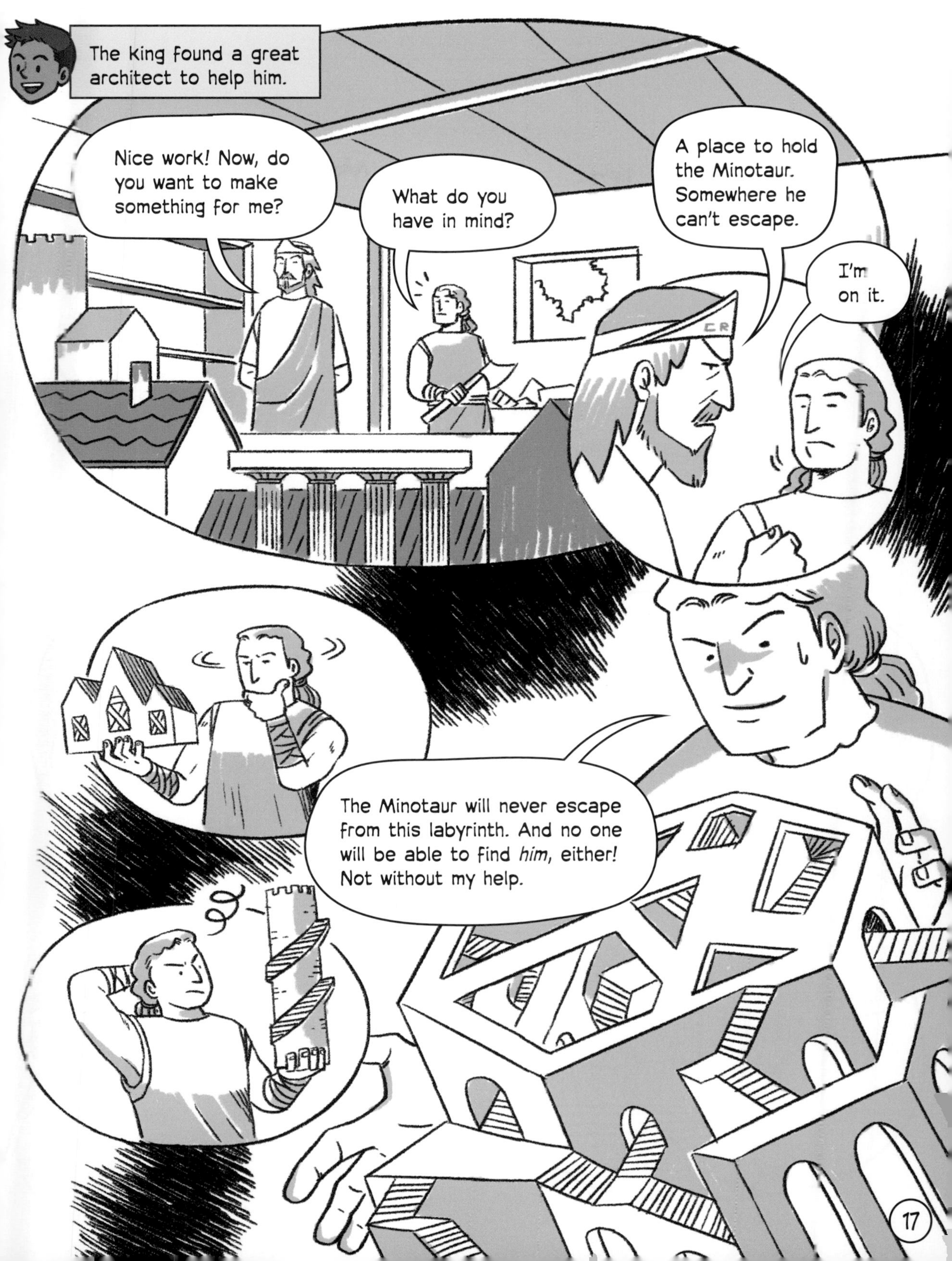
The king found a great architect to help him.
Nice work! Now, do you want to make something for me?
What do you have in mind?
A place to hold the Minotaur. Somewhere he can't escape.
I'm on it.
The Minotaur will never escape from this labyrinth. And no one will be able to find *him*, either! Not without my help.

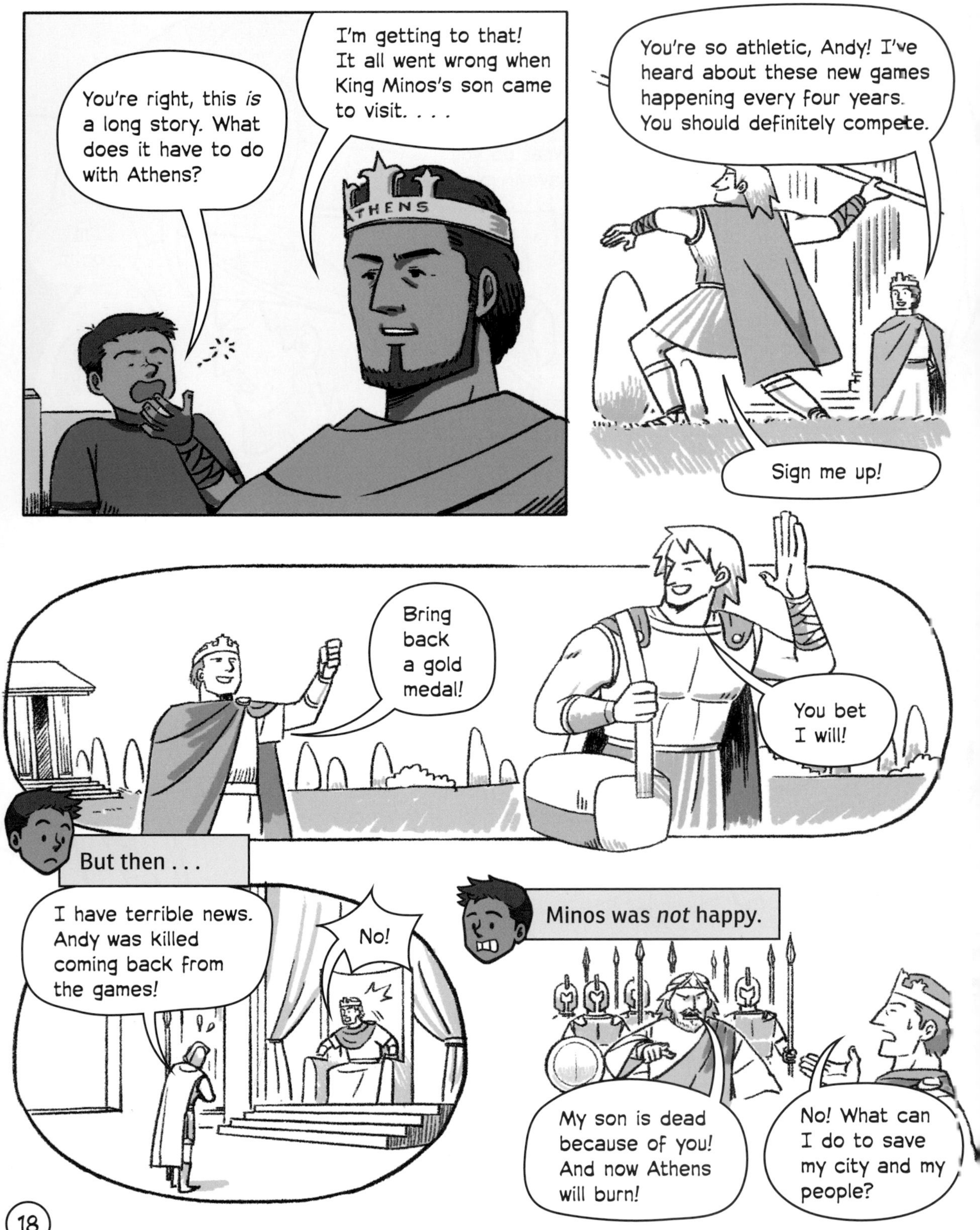

You're right, this *is* a long story. What does it have to do with Athens?
I'm getting to that! It all went wrong when King Minos's son came to visit. . . .
ATHENS
You're so athletic, Andy! I've heard about these new games happening every four years. You should definitely compete.
Sign me up!
Bring back a gold medal!
You bet I will!
But then . . .
I have terrible news. Andy was killed coming back from the games!
No!
Minos was *not* happy.
My son is dead because of you! And now Athens will burn!
No! What can I do to save my city and my people?

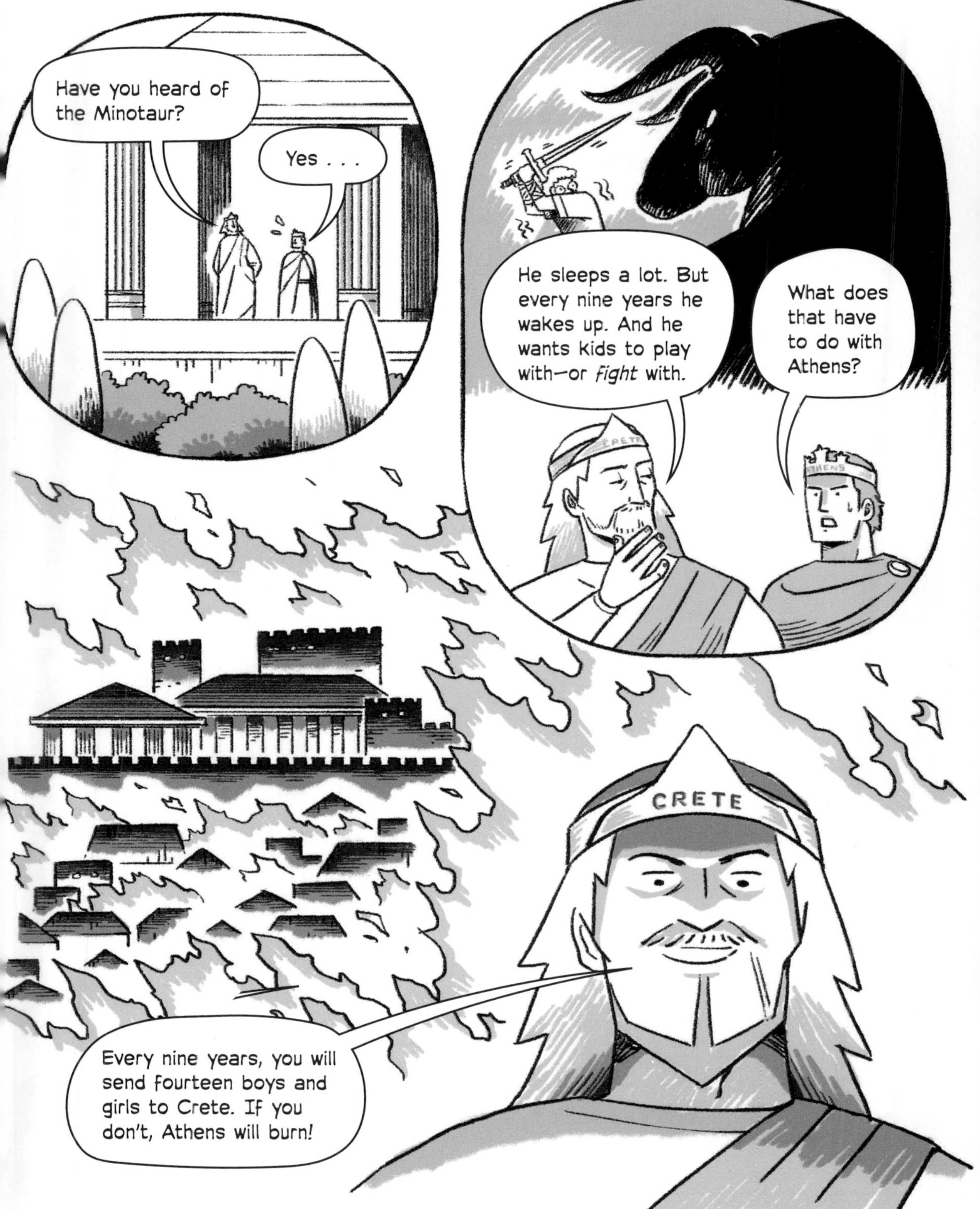
Have you heard of the Minotaur?
Yes . . .
He sleeps a lot. But every nine years he wakes up. And he wants kids to play with—or *fight* with.
What does that have to do with Athens?
CRETE
Every nine years, you will send fourteen boys and girls to Crete. If you don't, Athens will burn!

CHAPTER 3

A LITTLE HELP FROM MY FRIENDS

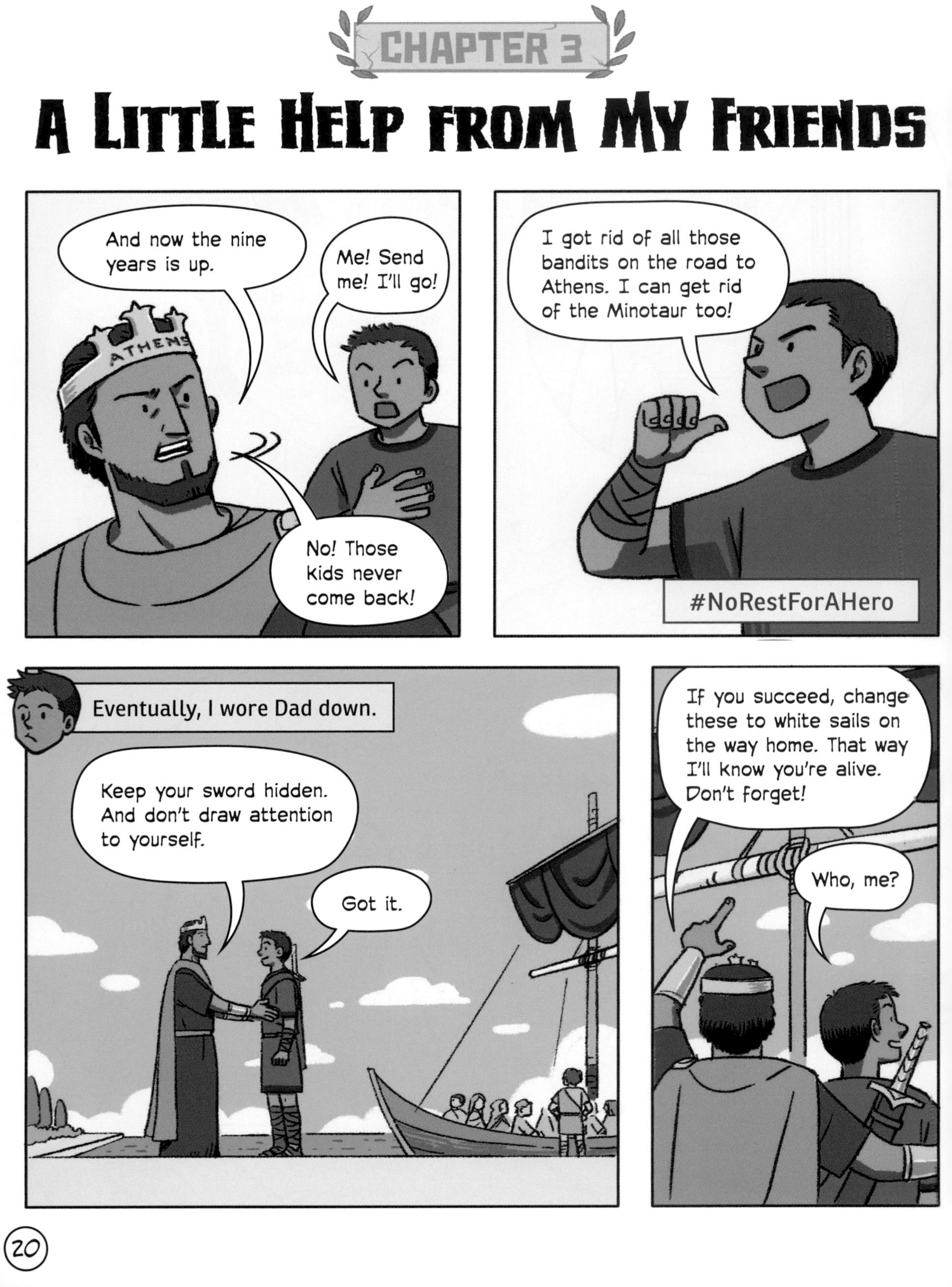

And now the nine years is up.
Me! Send me! I'll go!
ATHENS
No! Those kids never come back!
I got rid of all those bandits on the road to Athens. I can get rid of the Minotaur too!
#NoRestForAHero
Eventually, I wore Dad down.
Keep your sword hidden. And don't draw attention to yourself.
Got it.
If you succeed, change these to white sails on the way home. That way I'll know you're alive. Don't forget!
Who, me?

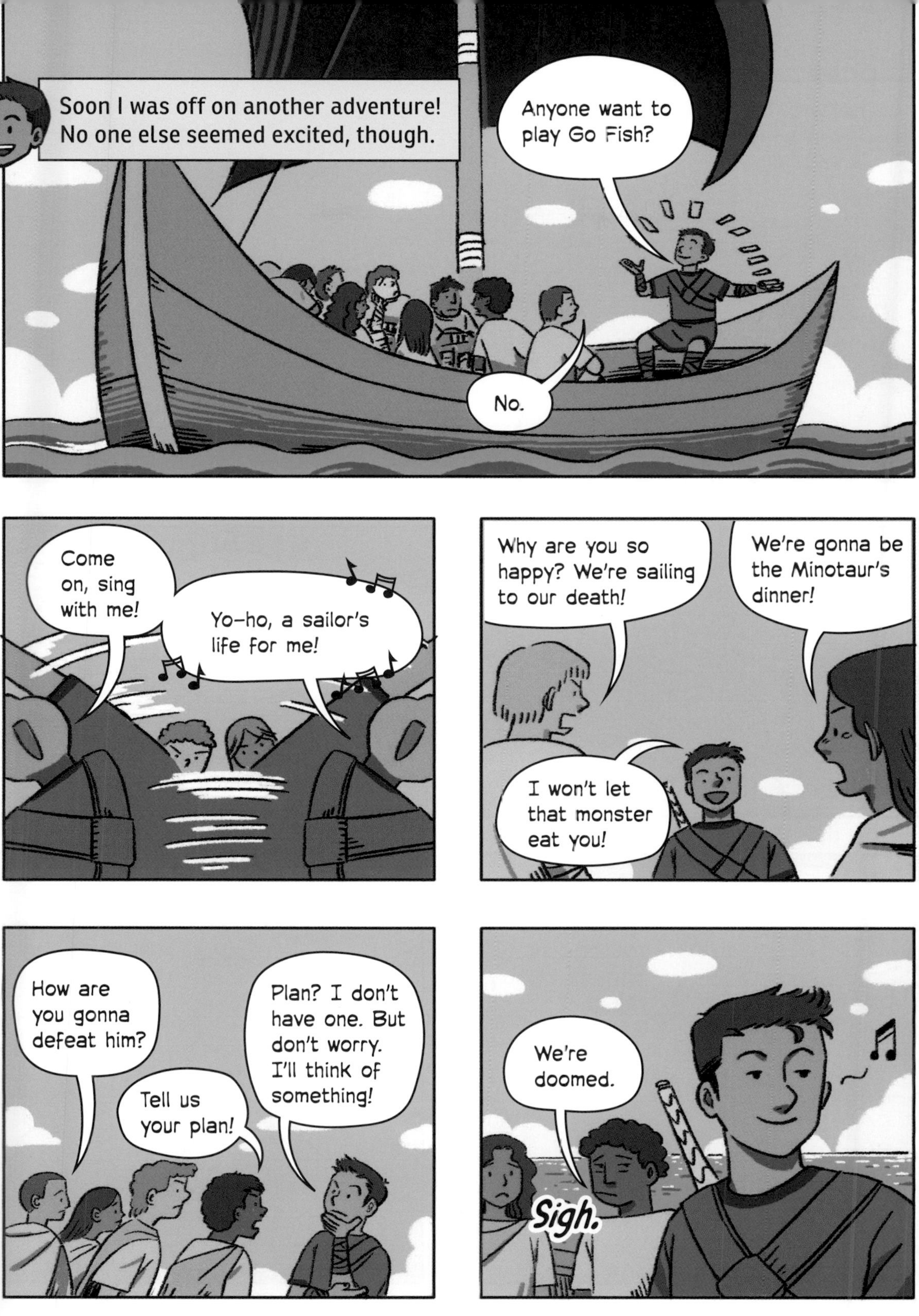
Soon I was off on another adventure! No one else seemed excited, though.
Anyone want to play Go Fish?
No.
Come on, sing with me!
Yo-ho, a sailor's life for me!
Why are you so happy? We're sailing to our death!
We're gonna be the Minotaur's dinner!
I won't let that monster eat you!
How are you gonna defeat him?
Tell us your plan!
Plan? I don't have one. But don't worry. I'll think of something!
We're doomed.
Sigh.

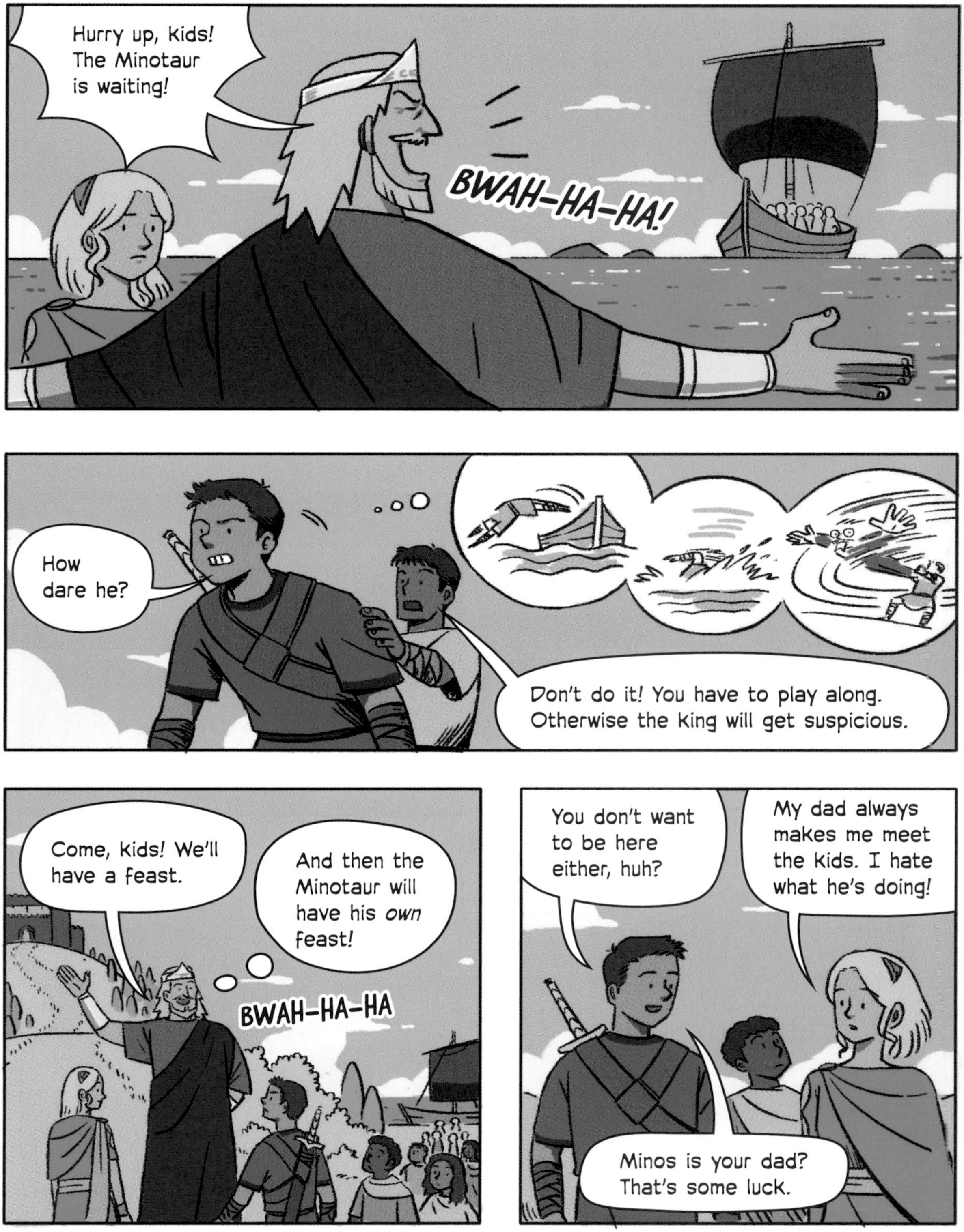
Hurry up, kids! The Minotaur is waiting!
BWAH-HA-HA!
How dare he?
Don't do it! You have to play along. Otherwise the king will get suspicious.
Come, kids! We'll have a feast.
And then the Minotaur will have his *own* feast!
BWAH-HA-HA
You don't want to be here either, huh?
My dad always makes me meet the kids. I hate what he's doing!
Minos is your dad? That's some luck.

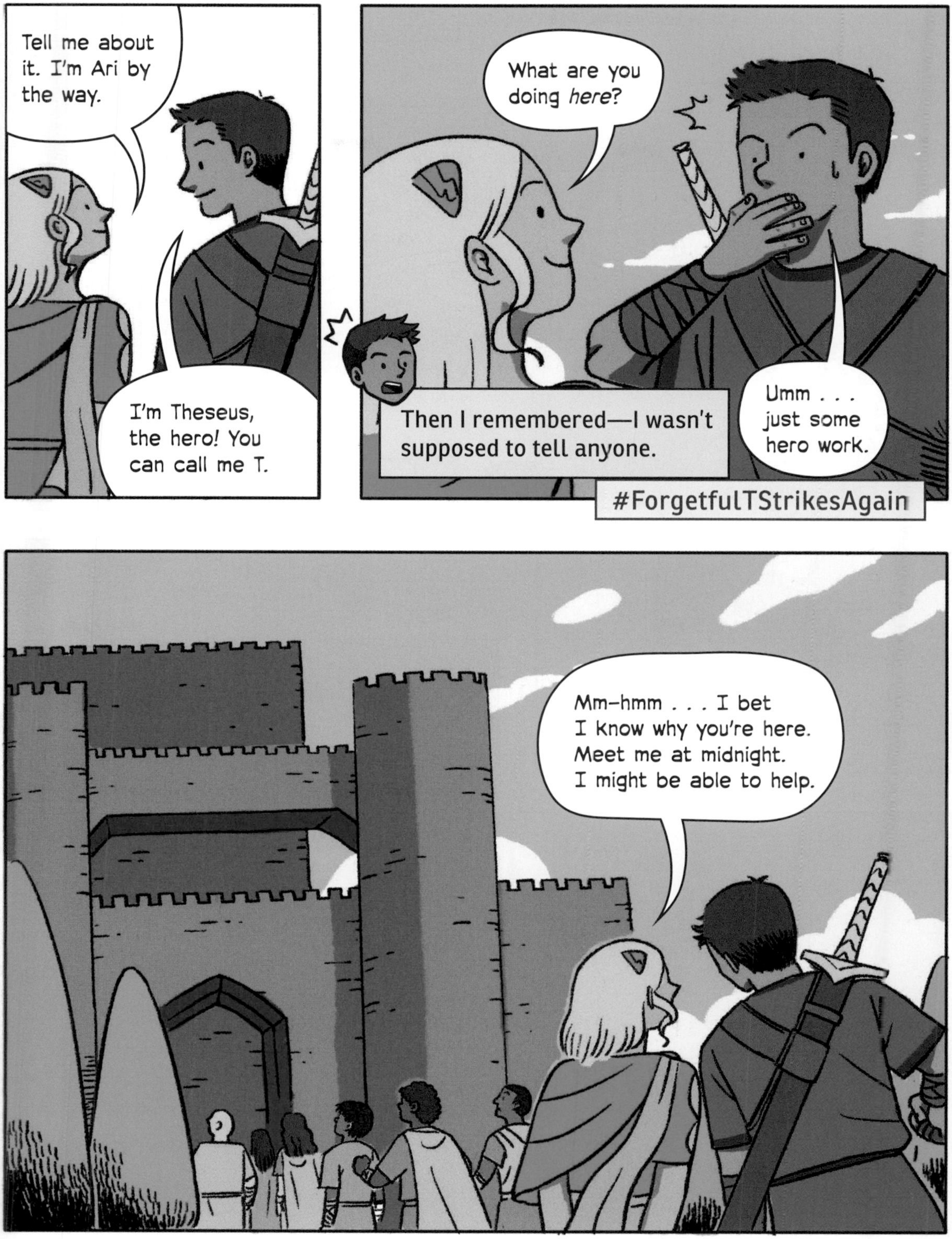

Tell me about it. I'm Ari by the way.
I'm Theseus, the hero! You can call me T.
What are you doing *here*?
Then I remembered—I wasn't supposed to tell anyone.
Umm . . . just some hero work.
#ForgetfulTStrikesAgain
Mm-hmm . . . I bet I know why you're here. Meet me at midnight. I might be able to help.

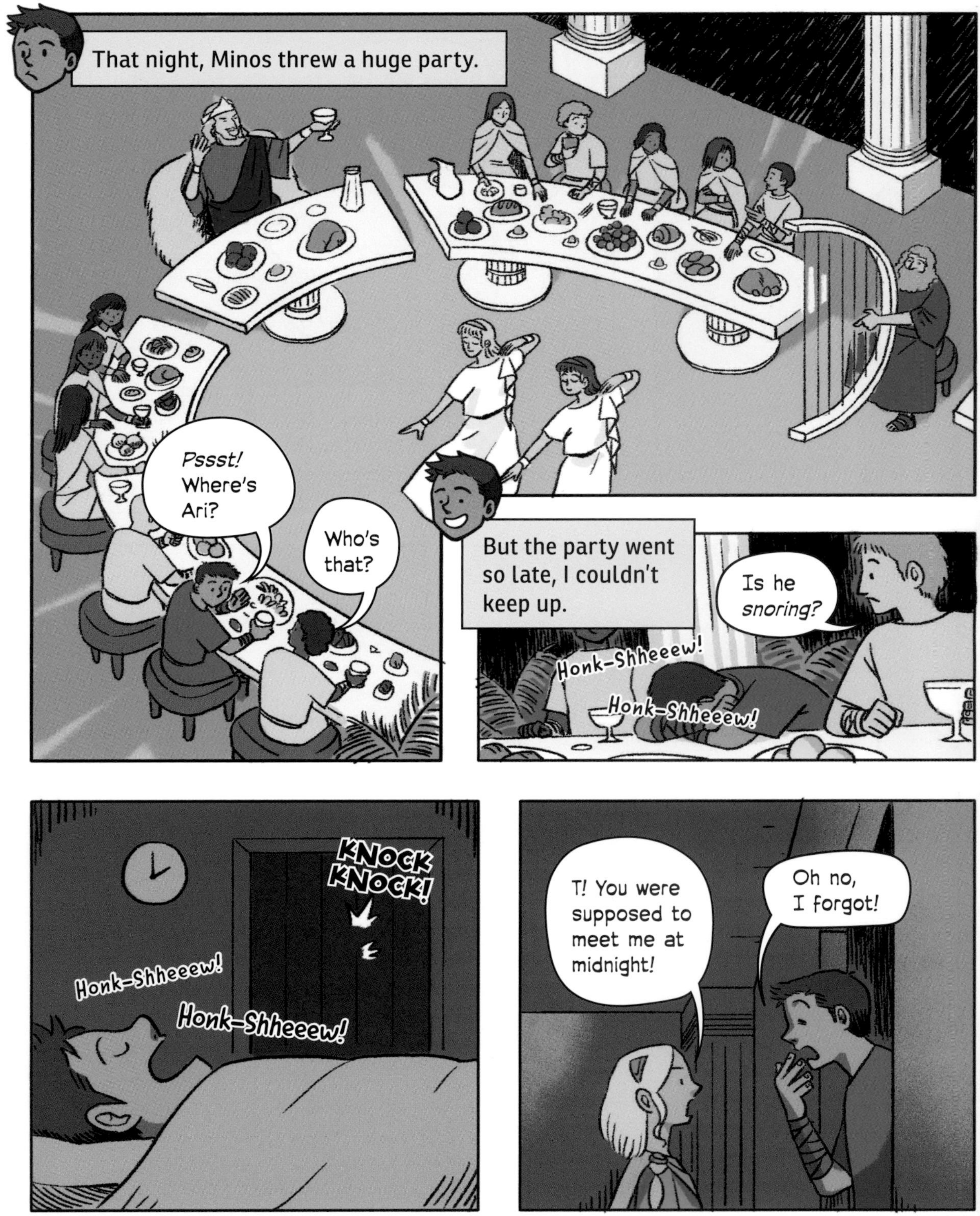
That night, Minos threw a huge party.
Pssst! Where's Ari?
Who's that?
But the party went so late, I couldn't keep up.
Is he snoring?
Honk-Shheeew!
Honk-Shheeew!
KNOCK KNOCK!
Honk-Shheeew!
Honk-Shheeew!
T! You were supposed to meet me at midnight!
Oh no, I forgot!

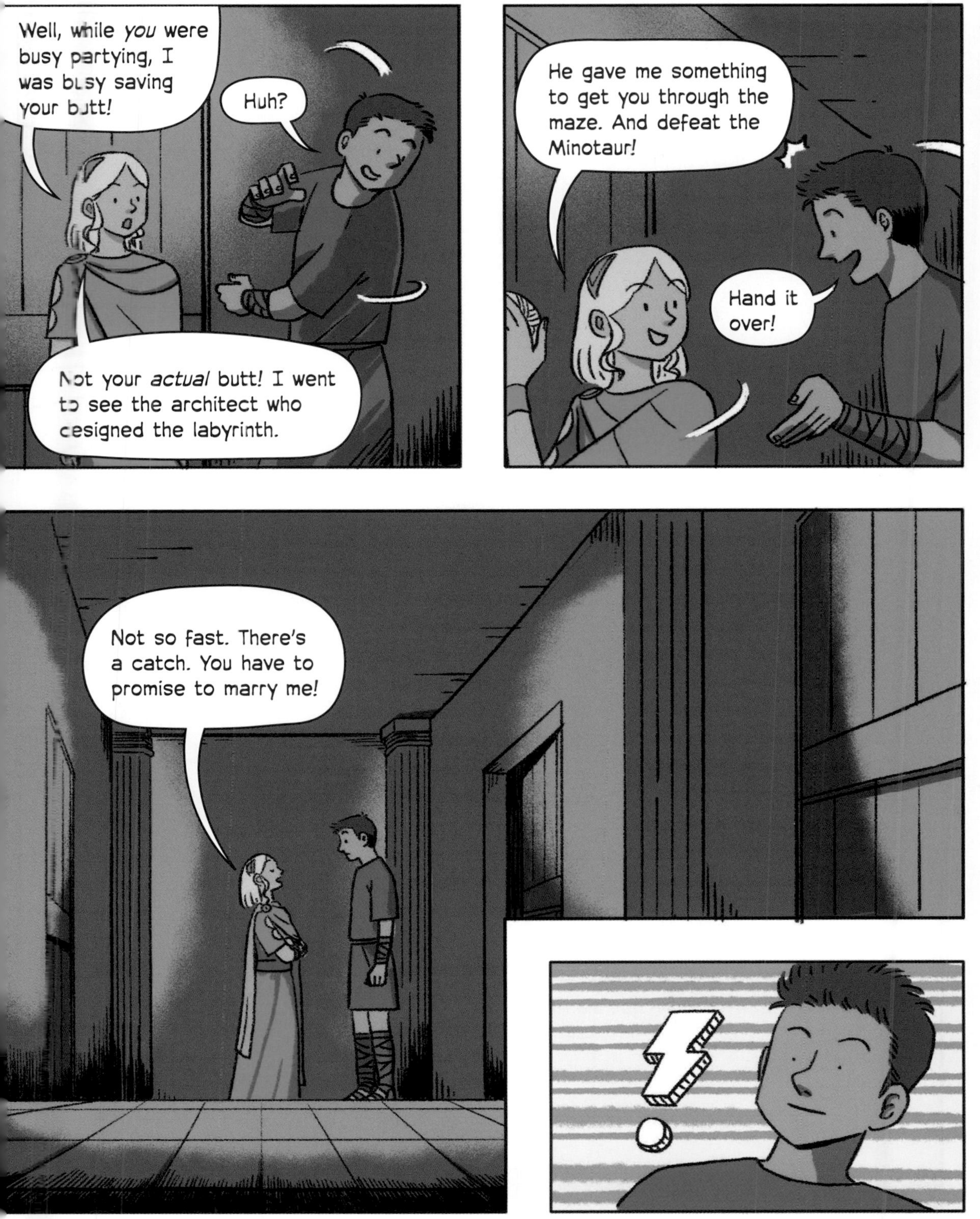
Well, while *you* were busy partying, I was busy saving your butt!
Huh?
Not your *actual* butt! I went to see the architect who designed the labyrinth.
He gave me something to get you through the maze. And defeat the Minotaur!
Hand it over!
Not so fast. There's a catch. You have to promise to marry me!

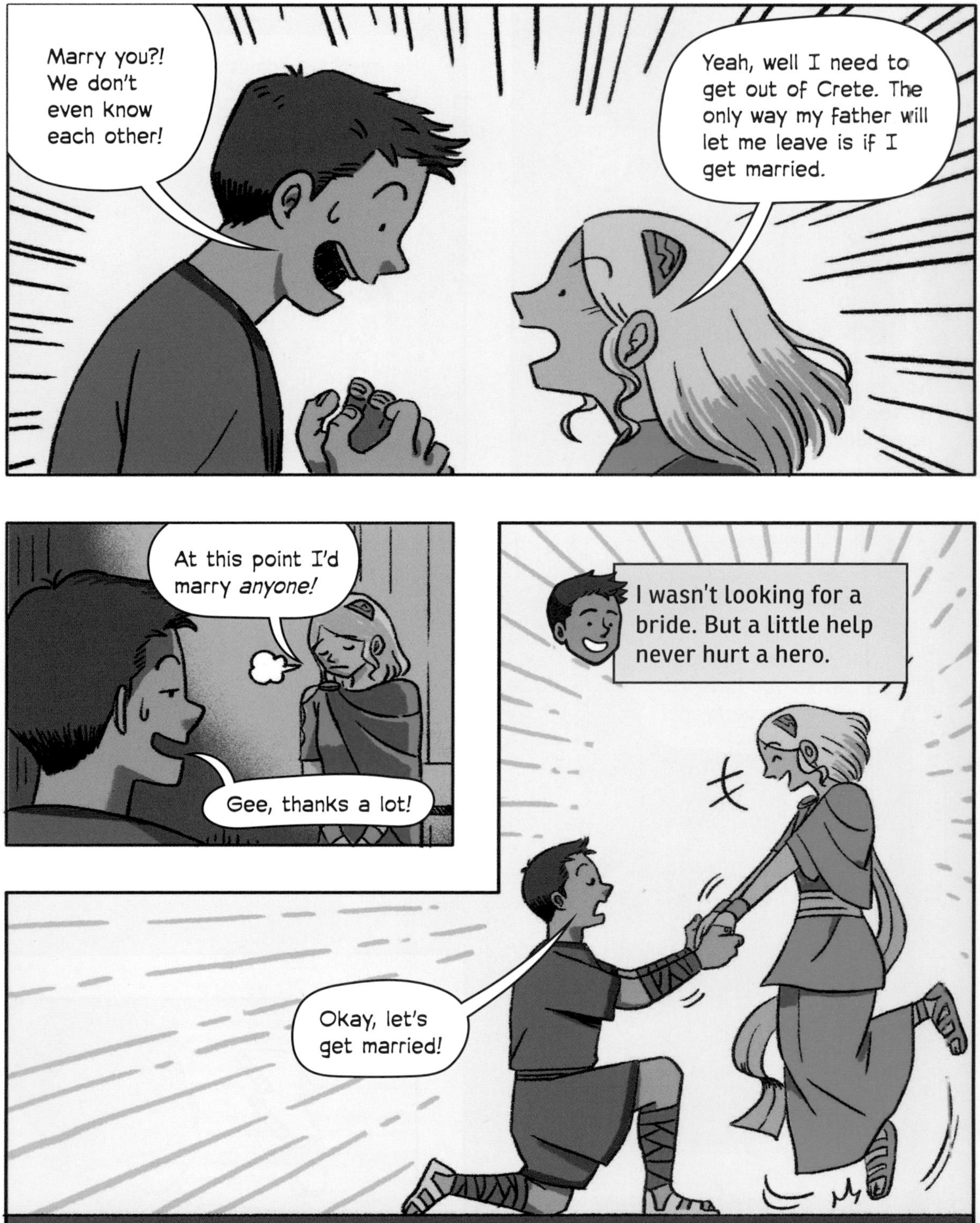
Marry you?! We don't even know each other!
Yeah, well I need to get out of Crete. The only way my father will let me leave is if I get married.
At this point I'd marry *anyone!*
Gee, thanks a lot!
I wasn't looking for a bride. But a little help never hurt a hero.
Okay, let's get married!

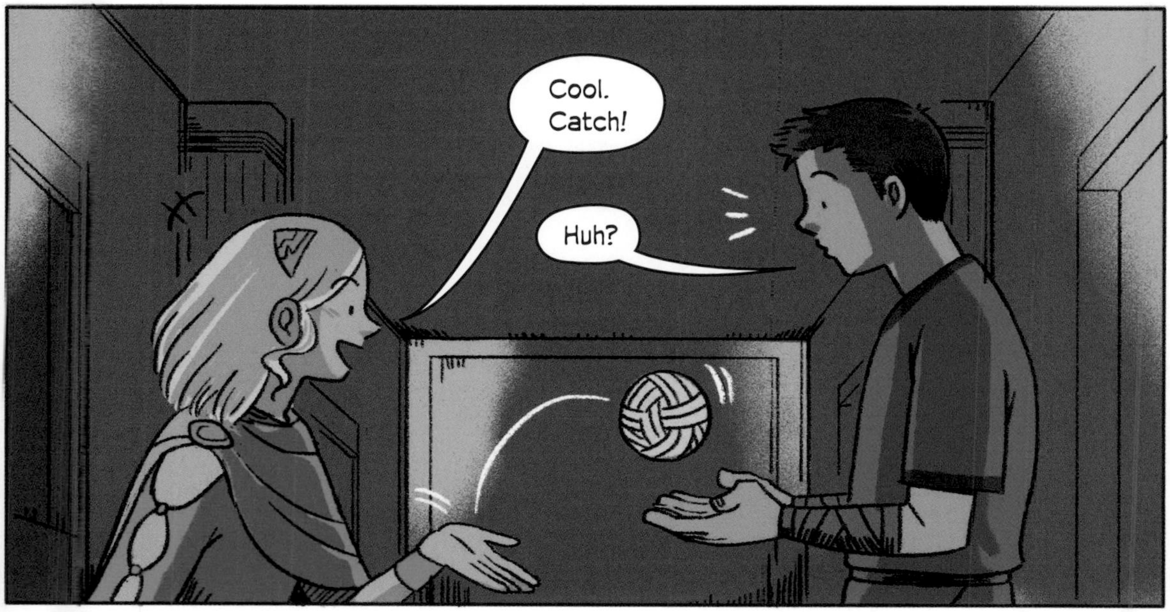
Cool. Catch!
Huh?

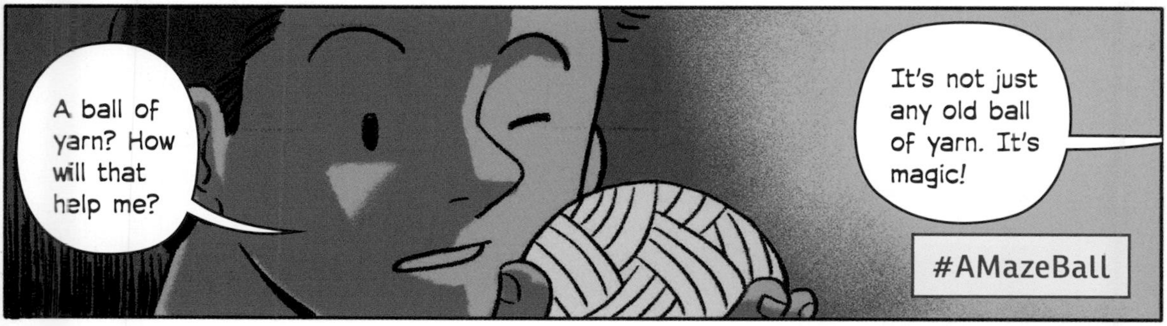
A ball of yarn? How will that help me?
It's not just any old ball of yarn. It's magic!
#AMazeBall

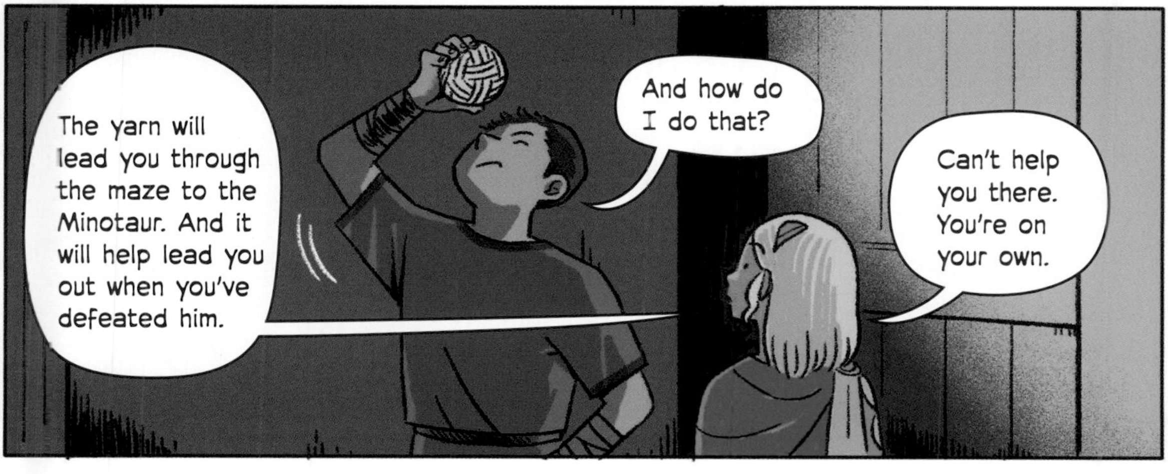
The yarn will lead you through the maze to the Minotaur. And it will help lead you out when you've defeated him.
And how do I do that?
Can't help you there. You're on your own.

CHAPTER 4

INTO THE MAZE

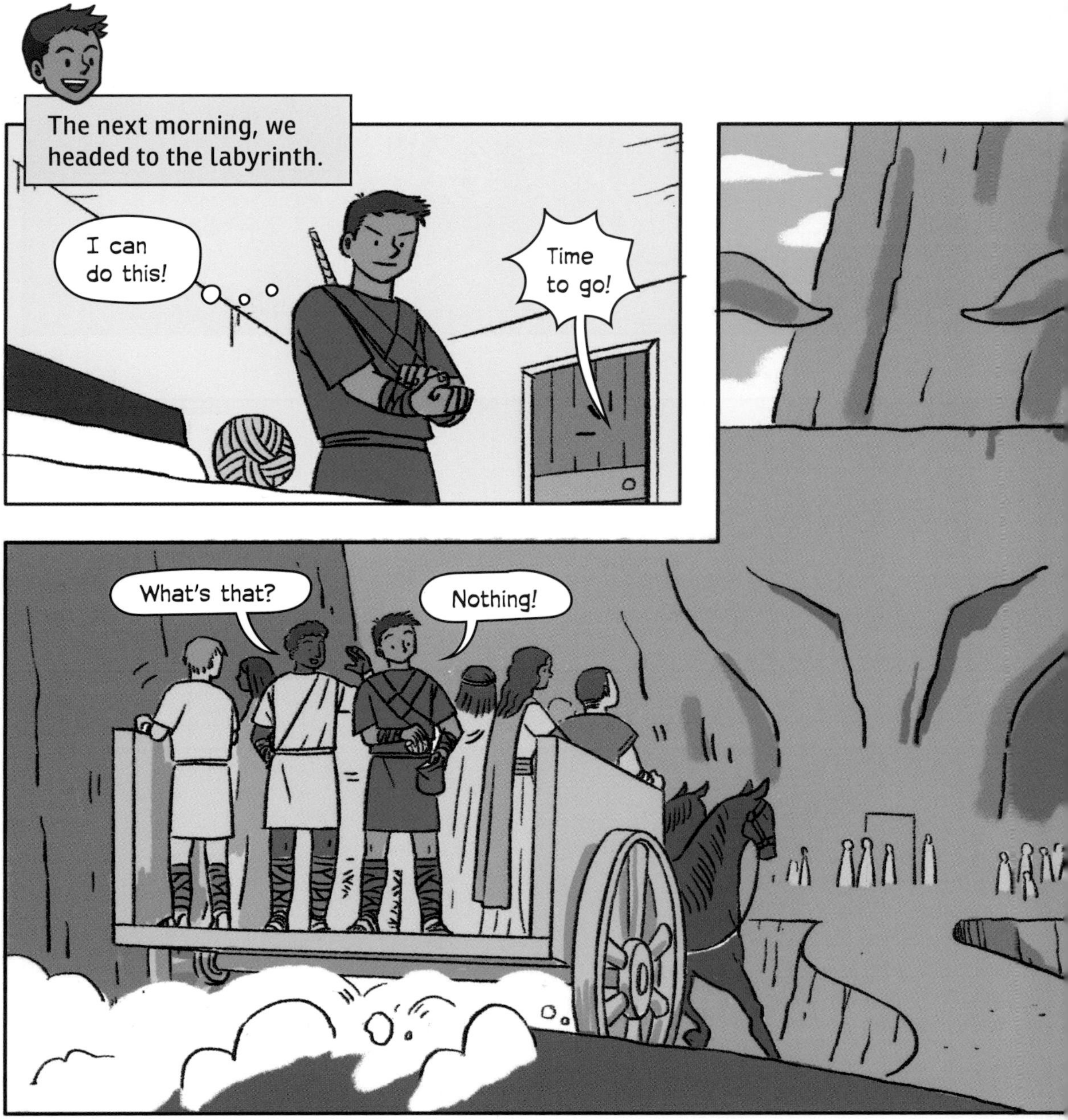
The next morning, we headed to the labyrinth.
I can do this!
Time to go!
What's that?
Nothing!

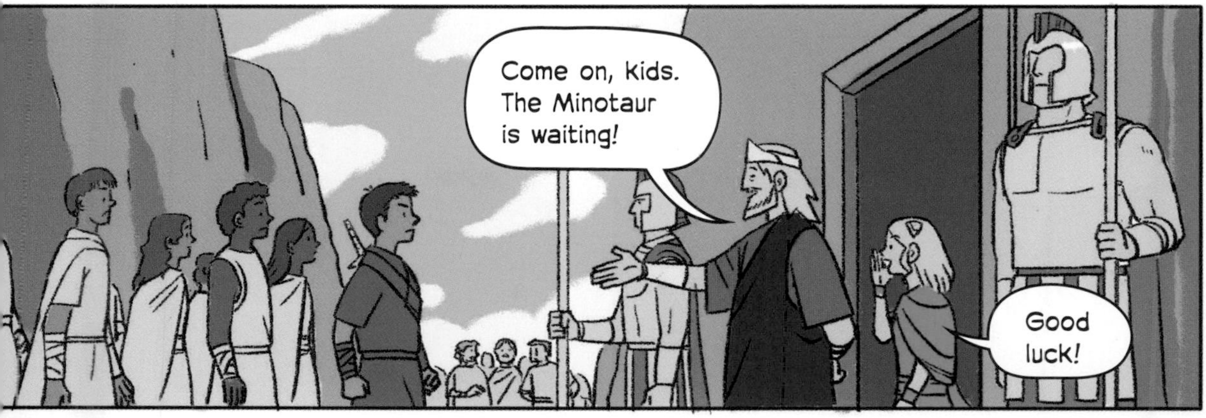
Come on, kids. The Minotaur is waiting!
Good luck!

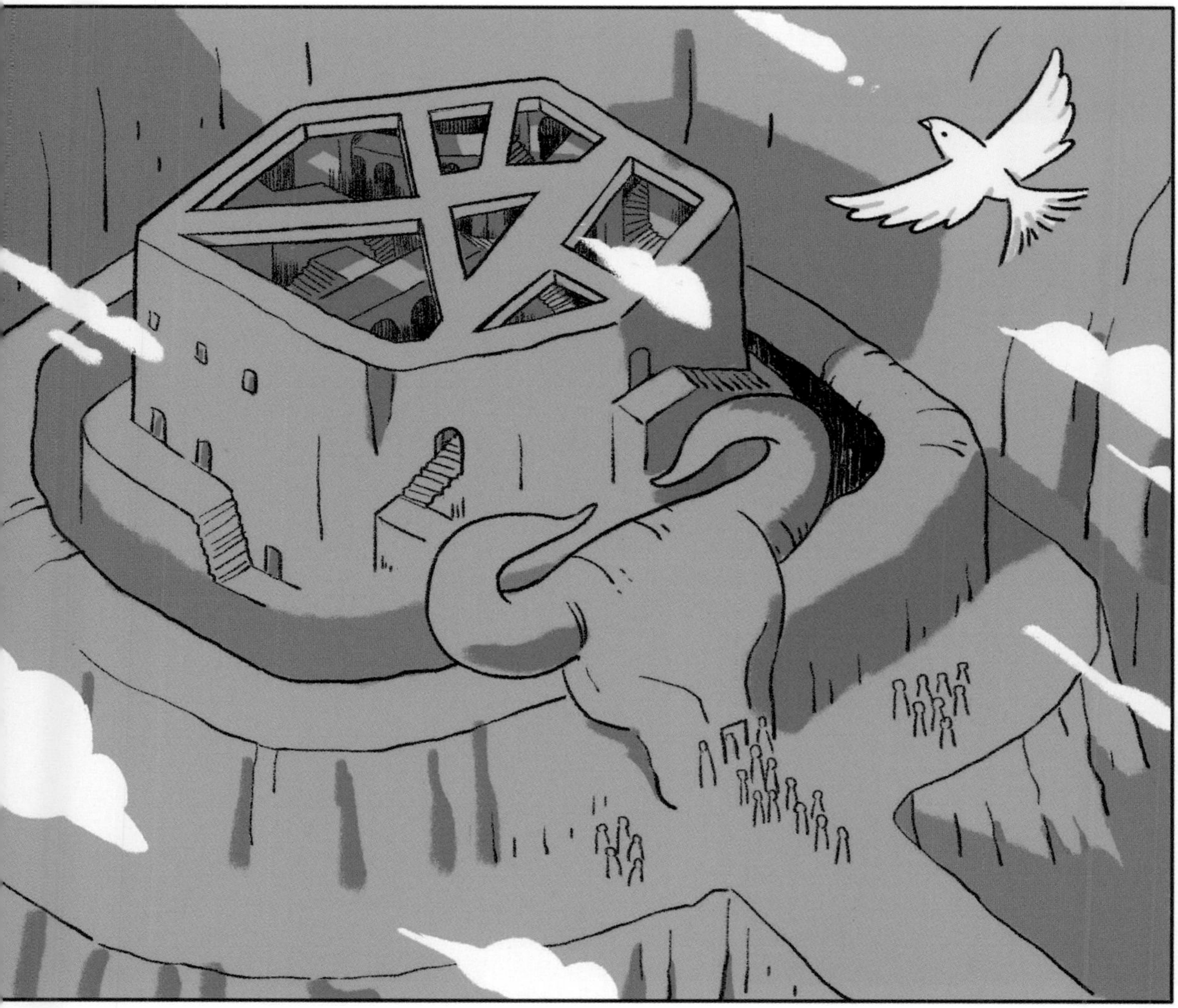

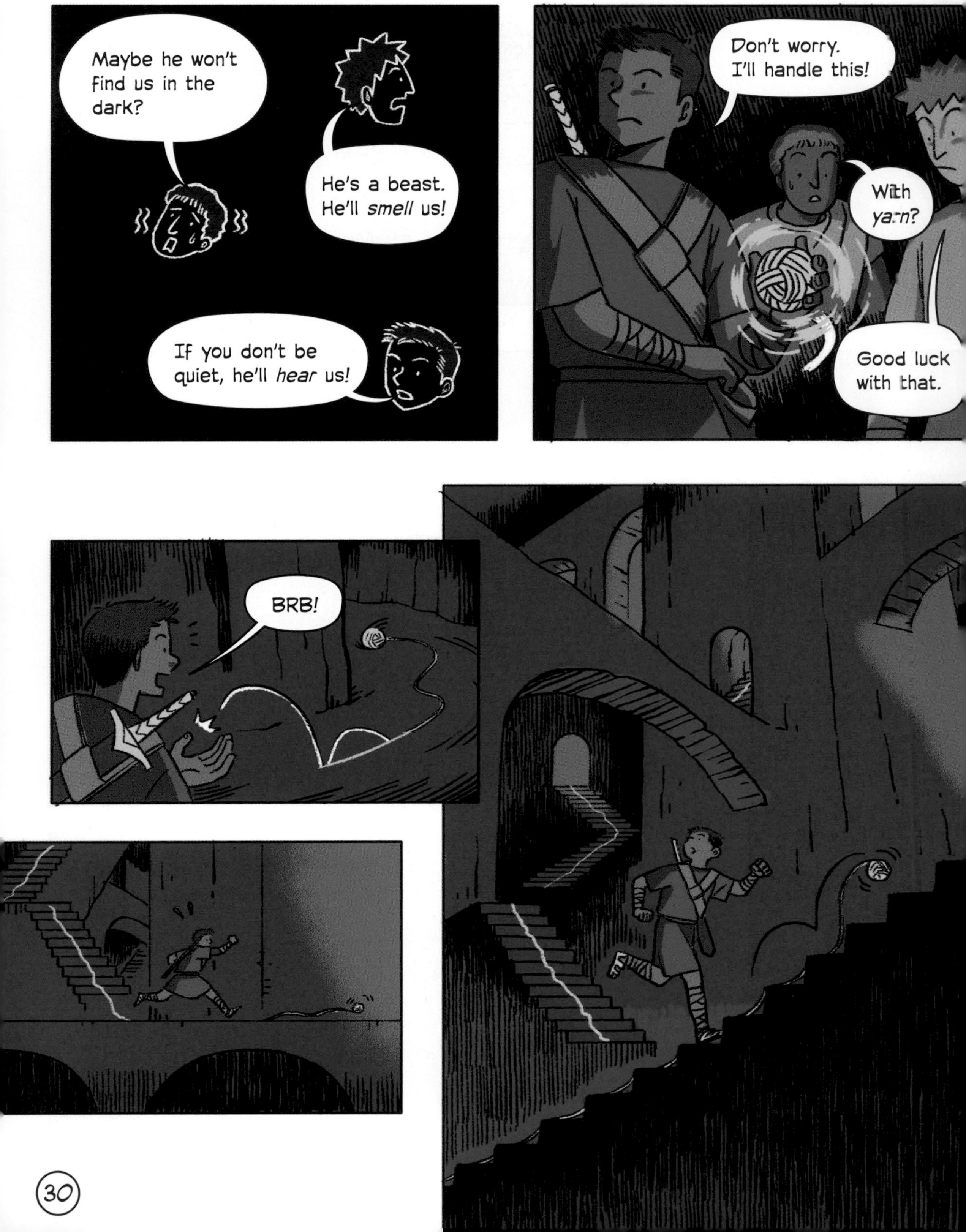
Maybe he won't find us in the dark?
He's a beast. He'll *smell* us!
If you don't be quiet, he'll *hear* us!
Don't worry. I'll handle this!
With *yarn*?
Good luck with that.
BRB!

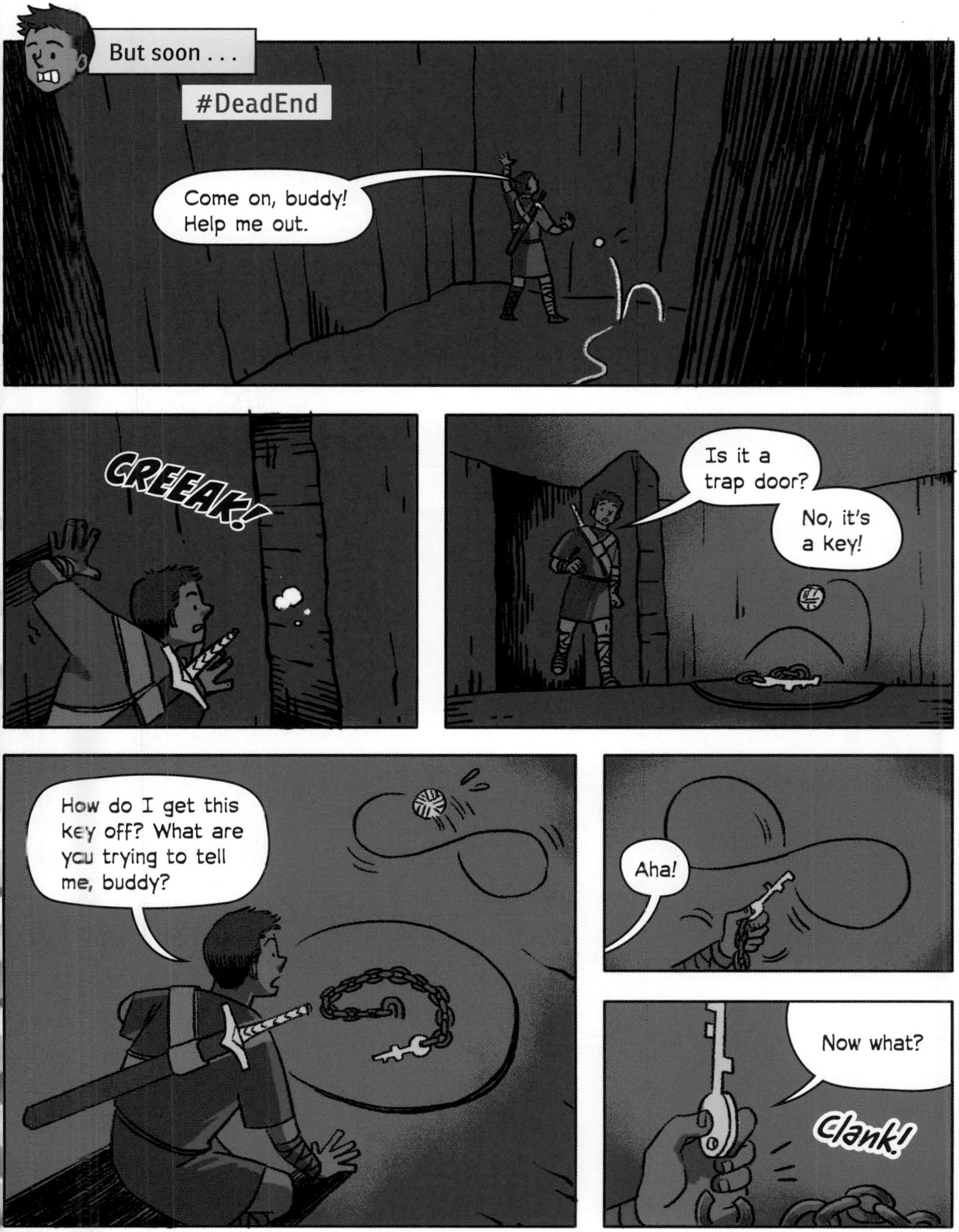
But soon . . .
#DeadEnd
Come on, buddy! Help me out.
CREEAK!
Is it a trap door?
No, it's a key!
How do I get this key off? What are you trying to tell me, buddy?
Aha!
Now what?
Clank!

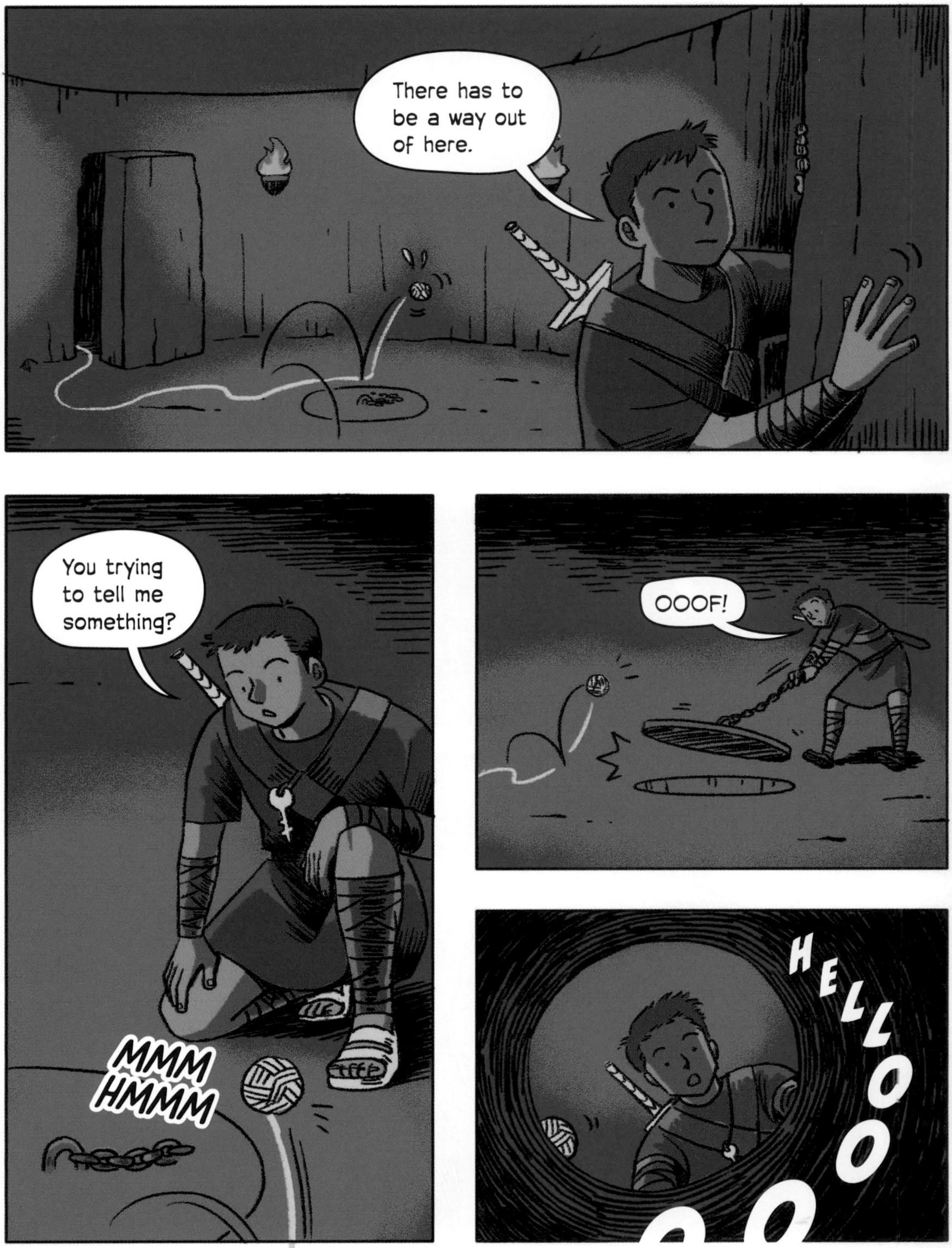
There has to be a way out of here.
You trying to tell me something?
MMM HMMM
OOOF!
HELLOOOOO

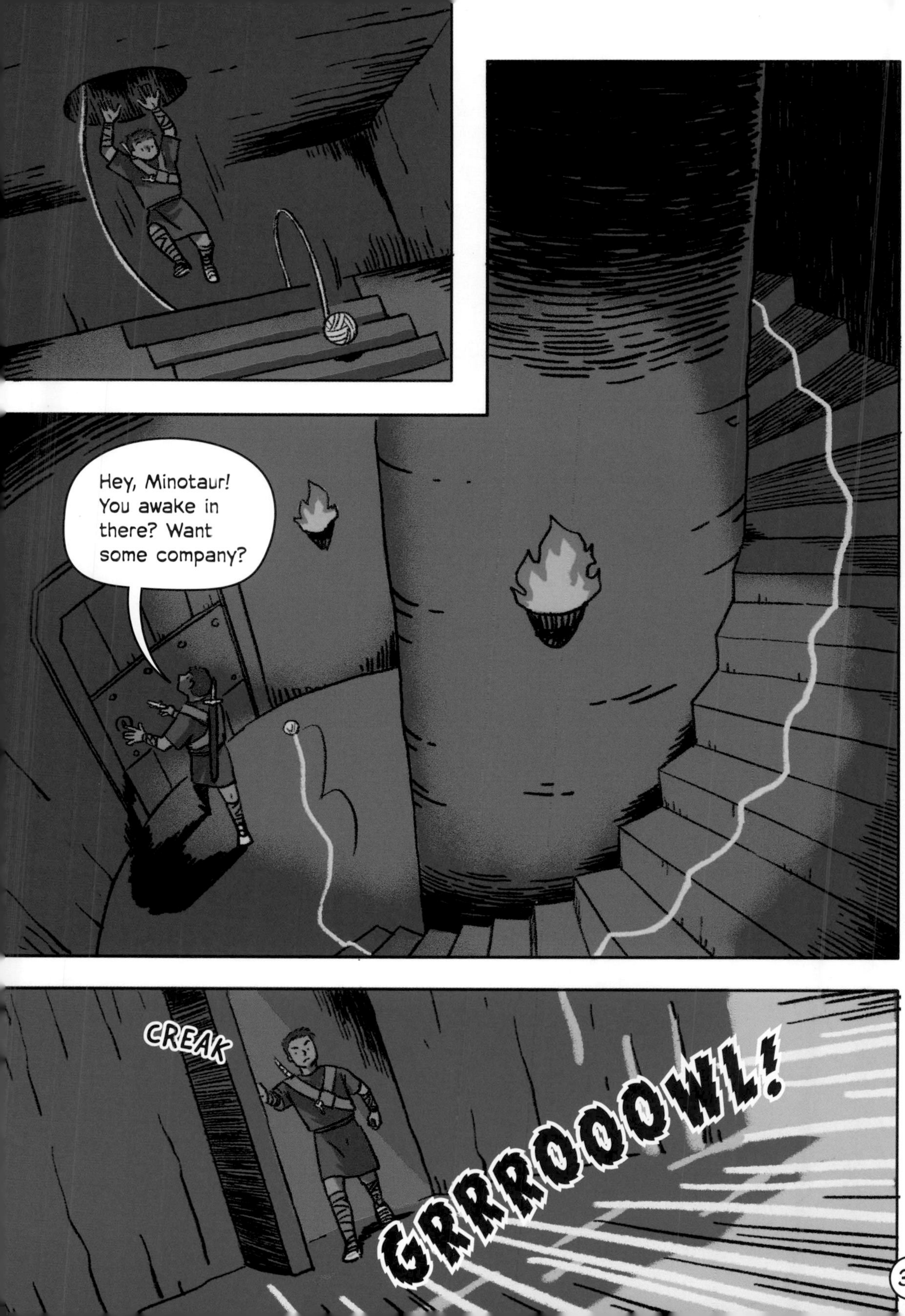

Hey, Minotaur! You awake in there? Want some company?
CREAK
GRRROOOOWL!

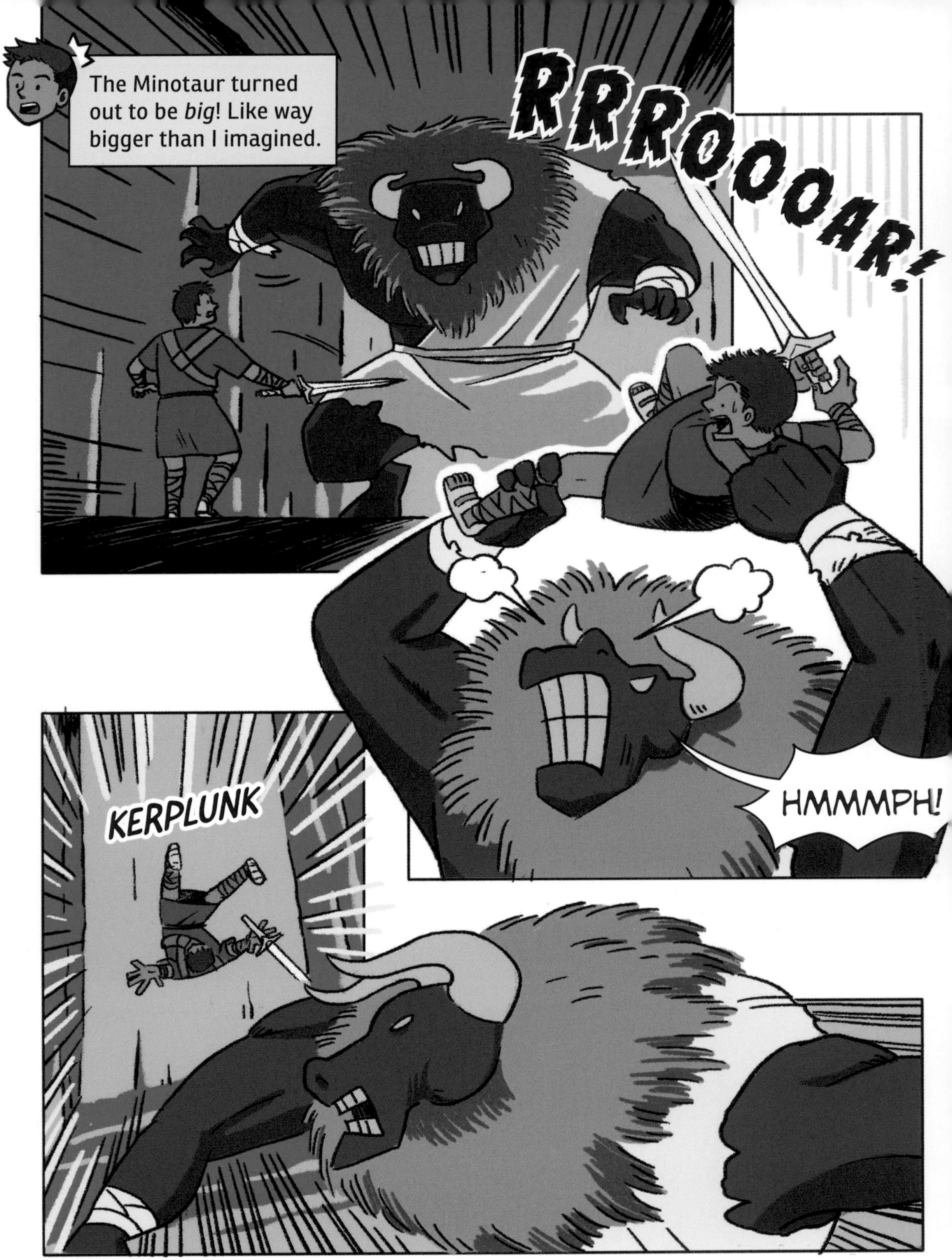
The Minotaur turned out to be *big*! Like way bigger than I imagined.
RRROOOOAR!
HMMMPH!
KERPLUNK

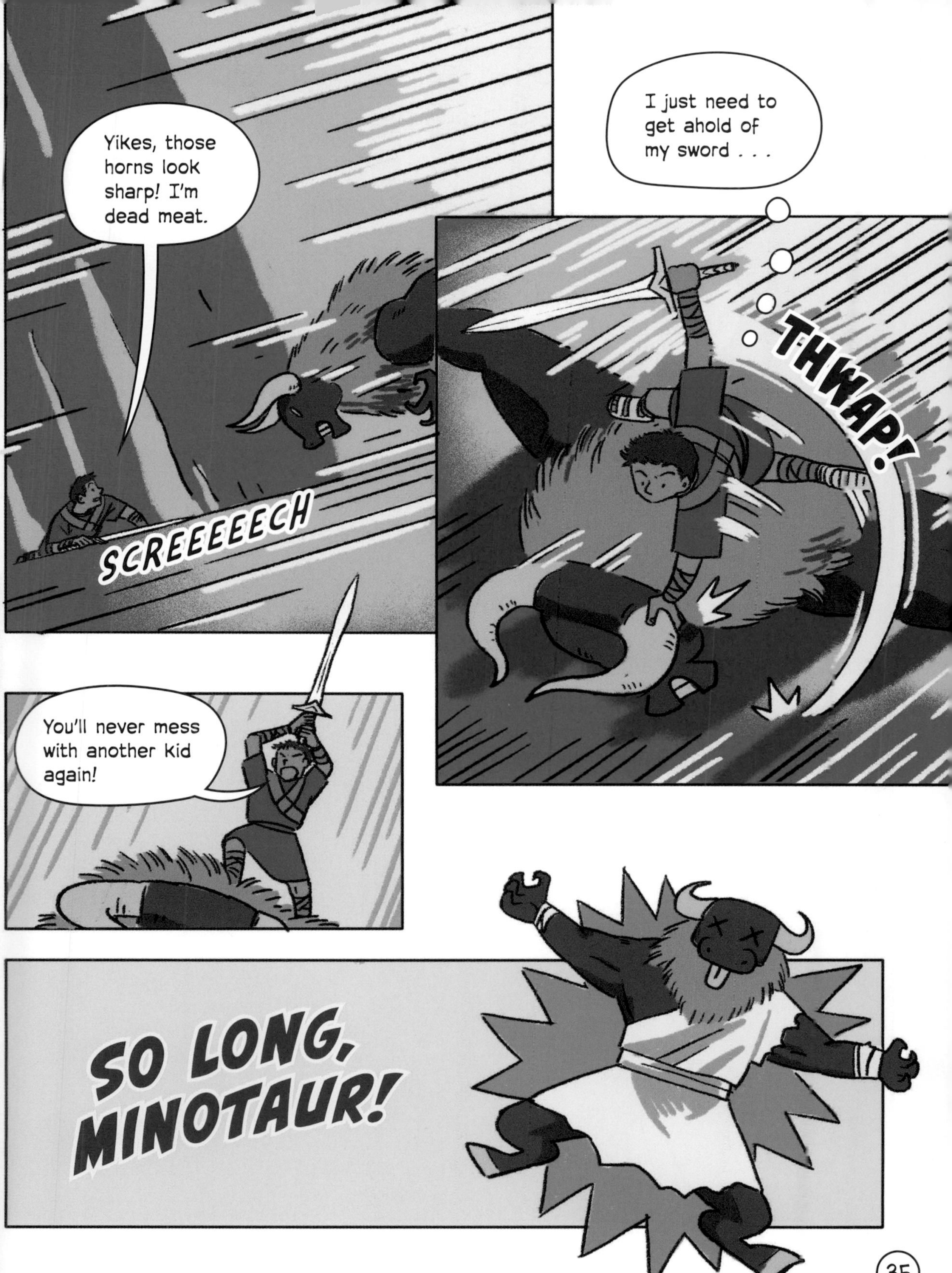
Yikes, those horns look sharp! I'm dead meat.
SCREEEEEECH
I just need to get ahold of my sword . . .
THWAP!
You'll never mess with another kid again!
SO LONG, MINOTAUR!

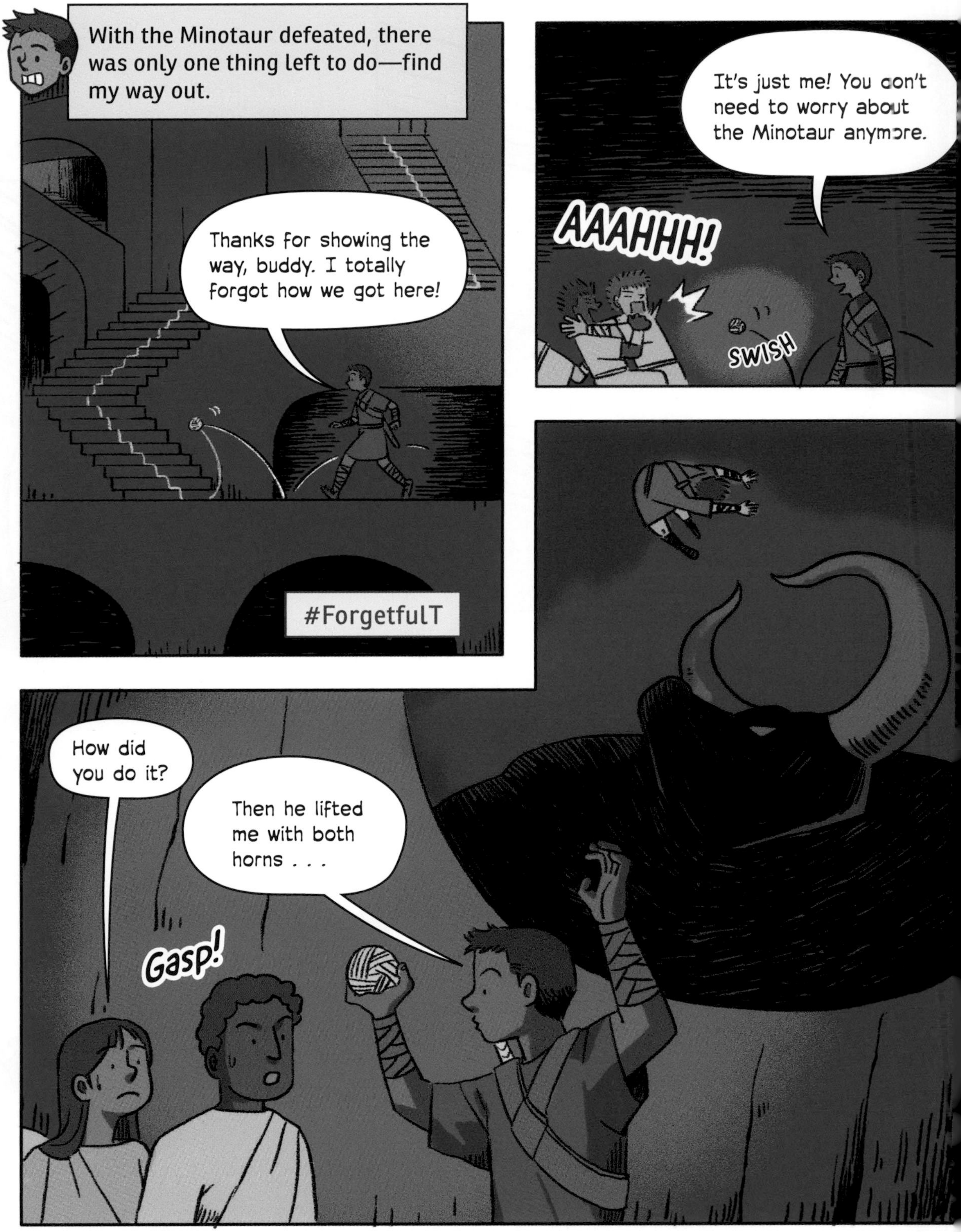
With the Minotaur defeated, there was only one thing left to do—find my way out.
Thanks for showing the way, buddy. I totally forgot how we got here!
#ForgetfulT
AAAHHH!
It's just me! You don't need to worry about the Minotaur anymore.
SWISH
How did you do it?
Gasp!
Then he lifted me with both horns . . .

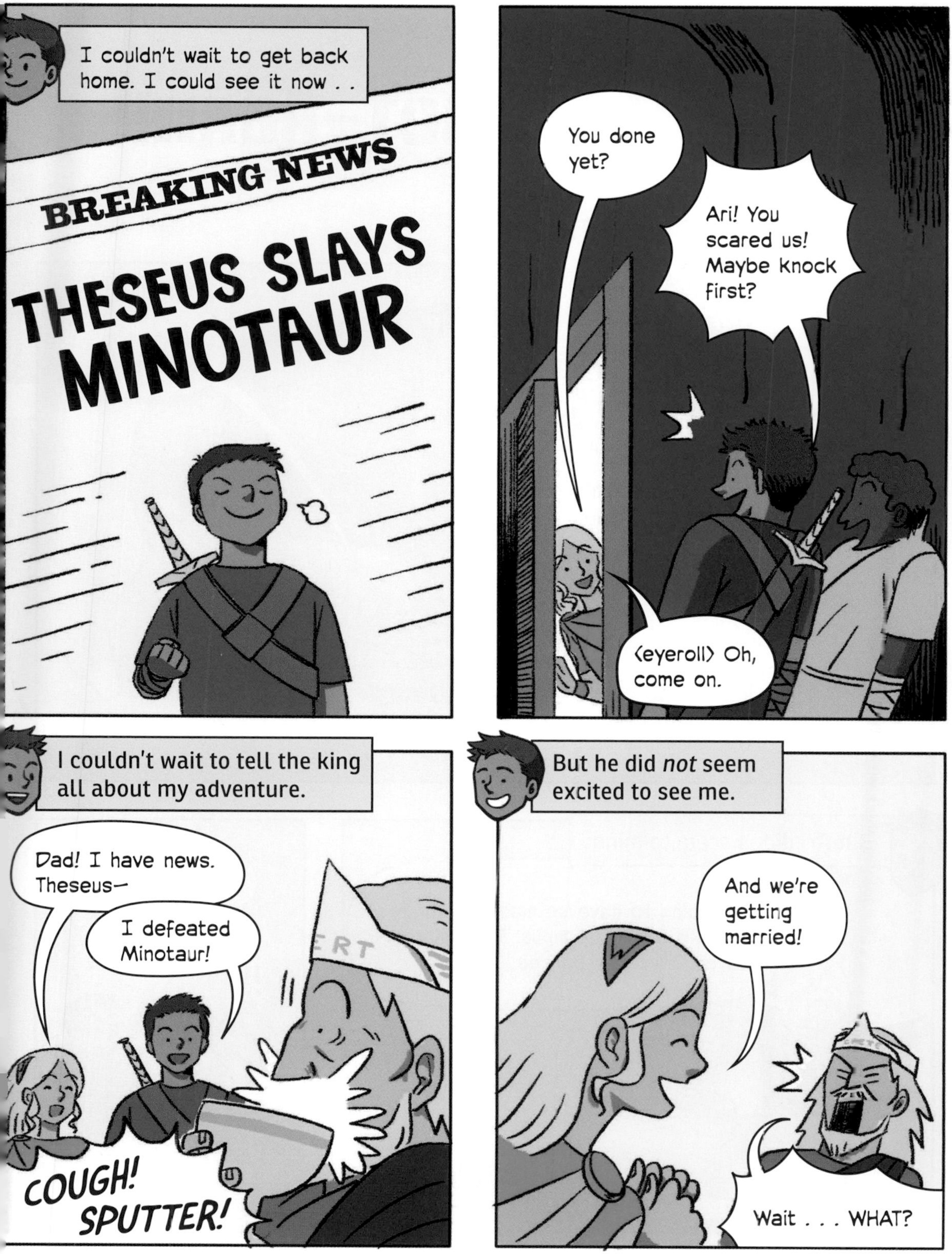
I couldn't wait to get back home. I could see it now . .
BREAKING NEWS
THESEUS SLAYS MINOTAUR
You done yet?
Ari! You scared us! Maybe knock first?
<eyeroll> Oh, come on.
I couldn't wait to tell the king all about my adventure.
Dad! I have news. Theseus—
I defeated Minotaur!
COUGH! SPUTTER!
But he did *not* seem excited to see me.
And we're getting married!
Wait . . . WHAT?

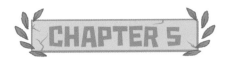

CHAPTER 5

OOPS, I FORGOT—AGAIN!

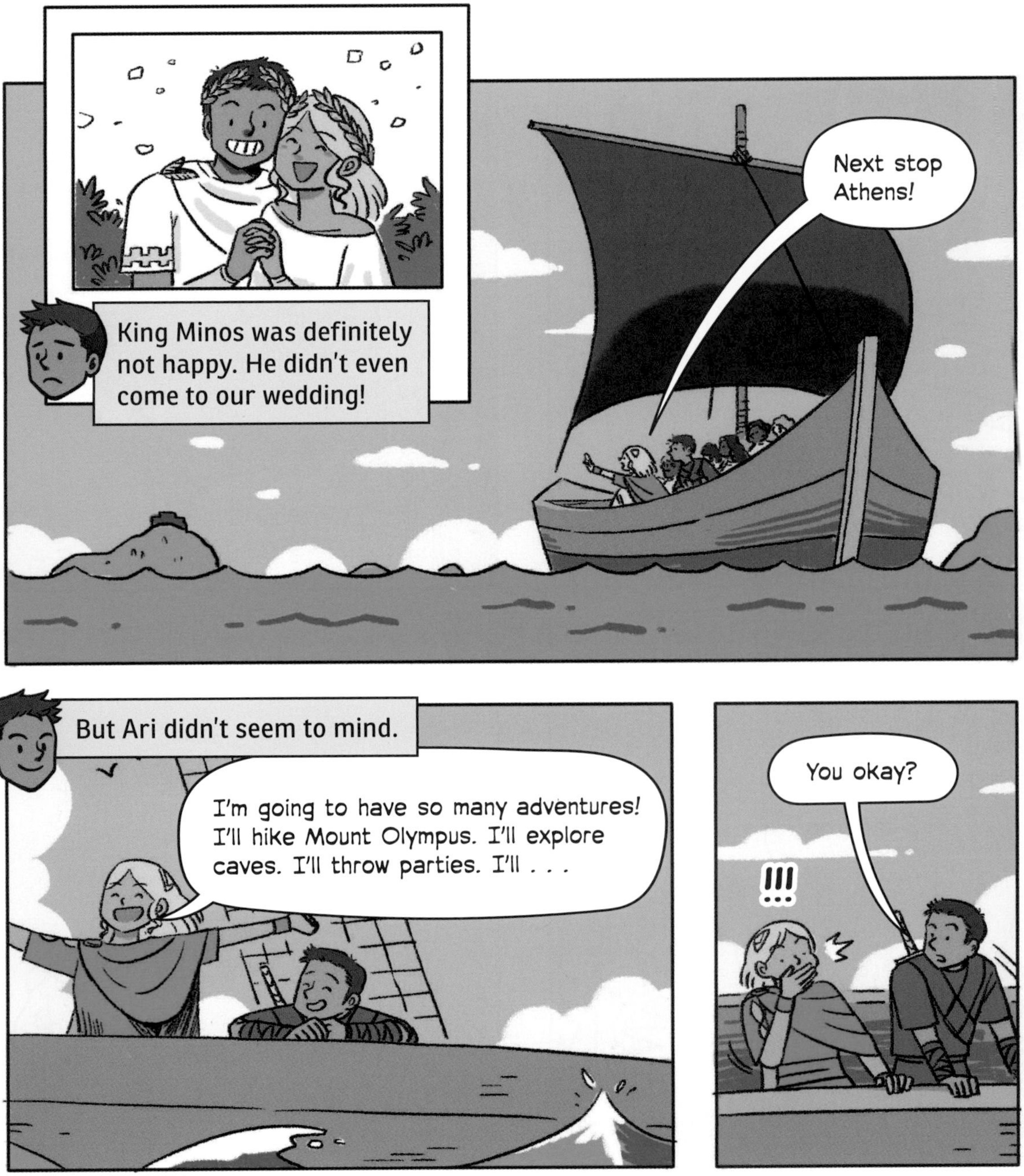
King Minos was definitely not happy. He didn't even come to our wedding!
Next stop Athens!
But Ari didn't seem to mind.
I'm going to have so many adventures! I'll hike Mount Olympus. I'll explore caves. I'll throw parties. I'll . . .
You okay?
!!!

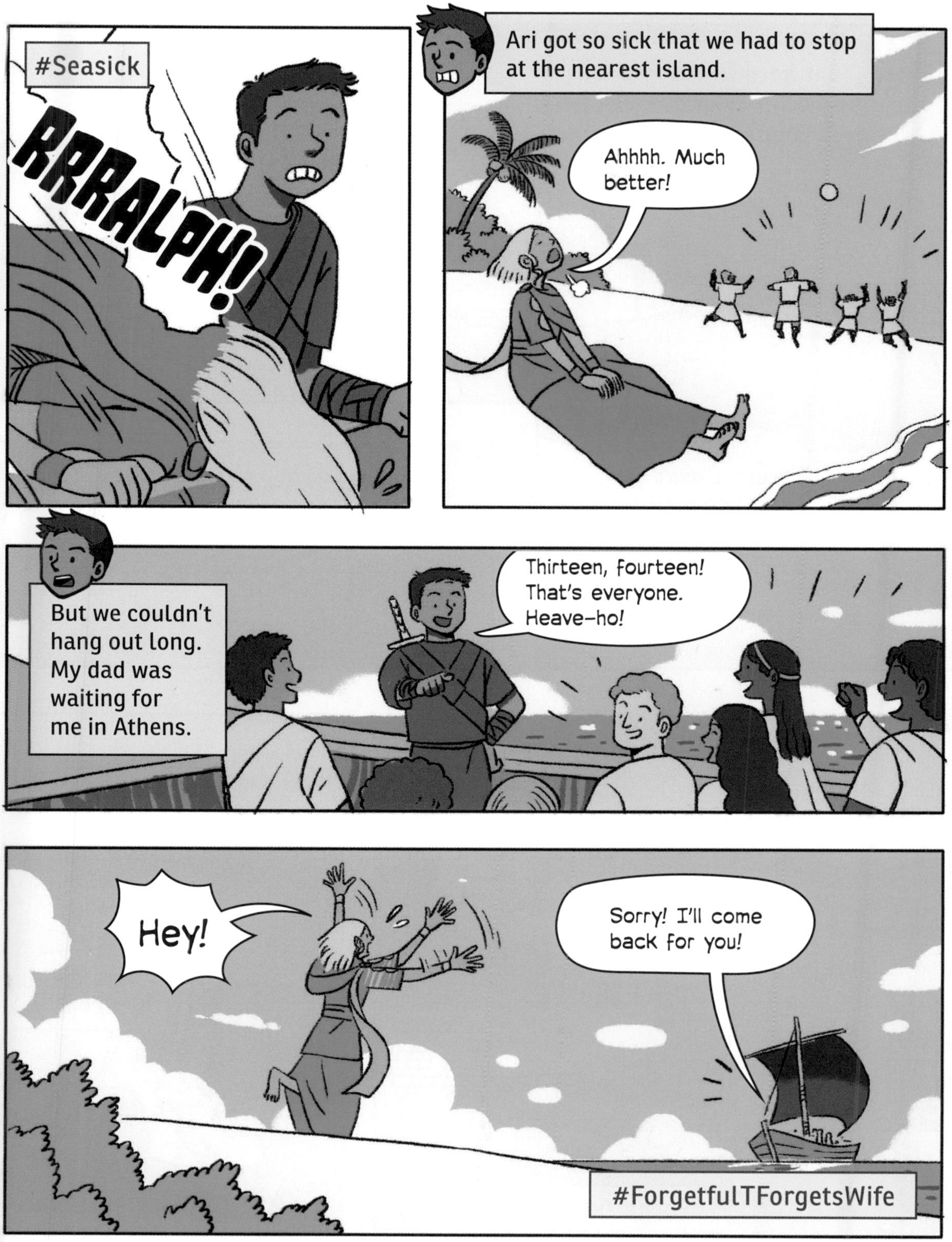
#Seasick
RRRALPH!
Ari got so sick that we had to stop at the nearest island.
Ahhhh. Much better!
But we couldn't hang out long. My dad was waiting for me in Athens.
Thirteen, fourteen! That's everyone. Heave-ho!
Hey!
Sorry! I'll come back for you!
#ForgetfulTForgetsWife

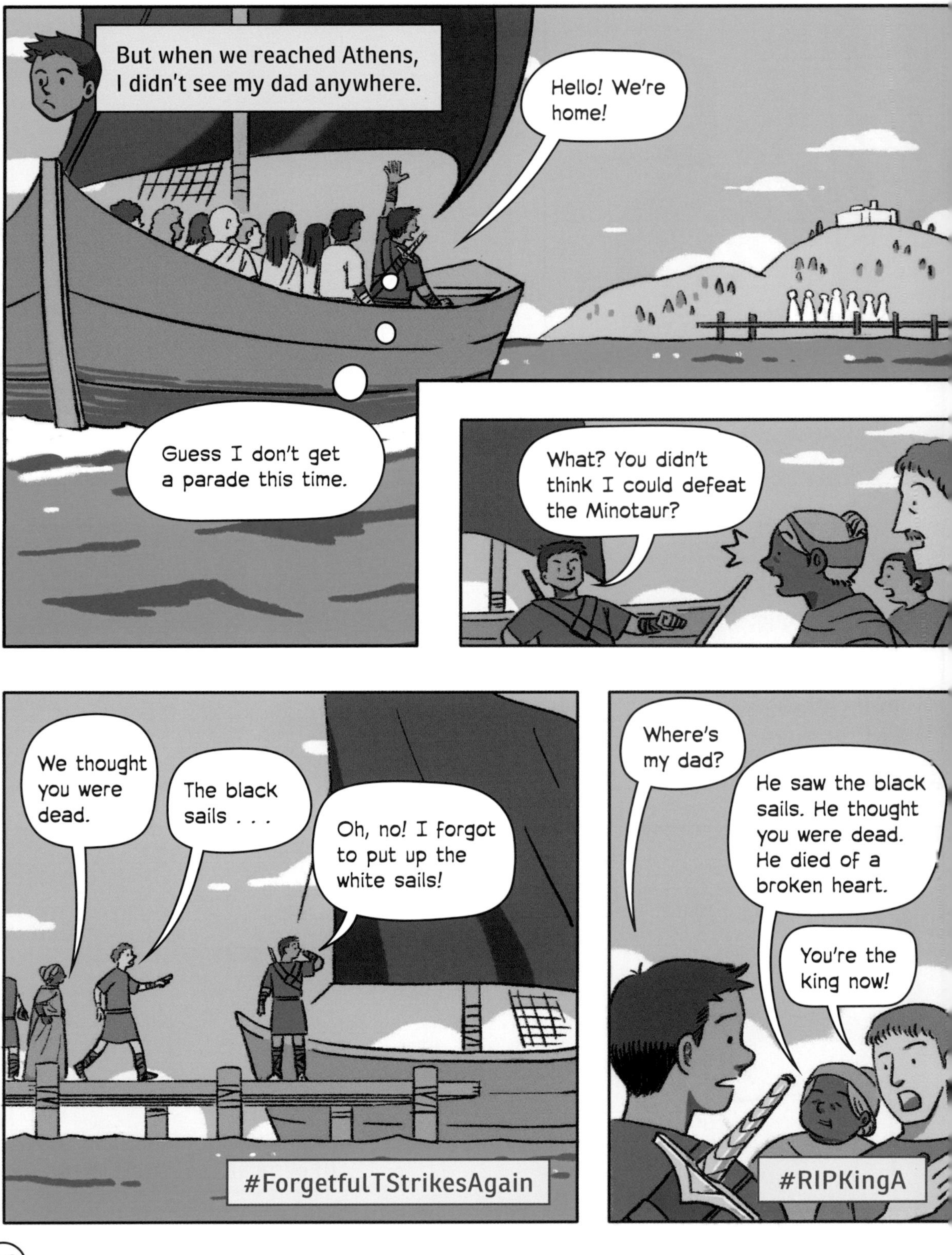

But when we reached Athens, I didn't see my dad anywhere.
Hello! We're home!
Guess I don't get a parade this time.
What? You didn't think I could defeat the Minotaur?
We thought you were dead.
The black sails . . .
Oh, no! I forgot to put up the white sails!
#ForgetfulTStrikesAgain
Where's my dad?
He saw the black sails. He thought you were dead. He died of a broken heart.
You're the King now!
#RIPKingA

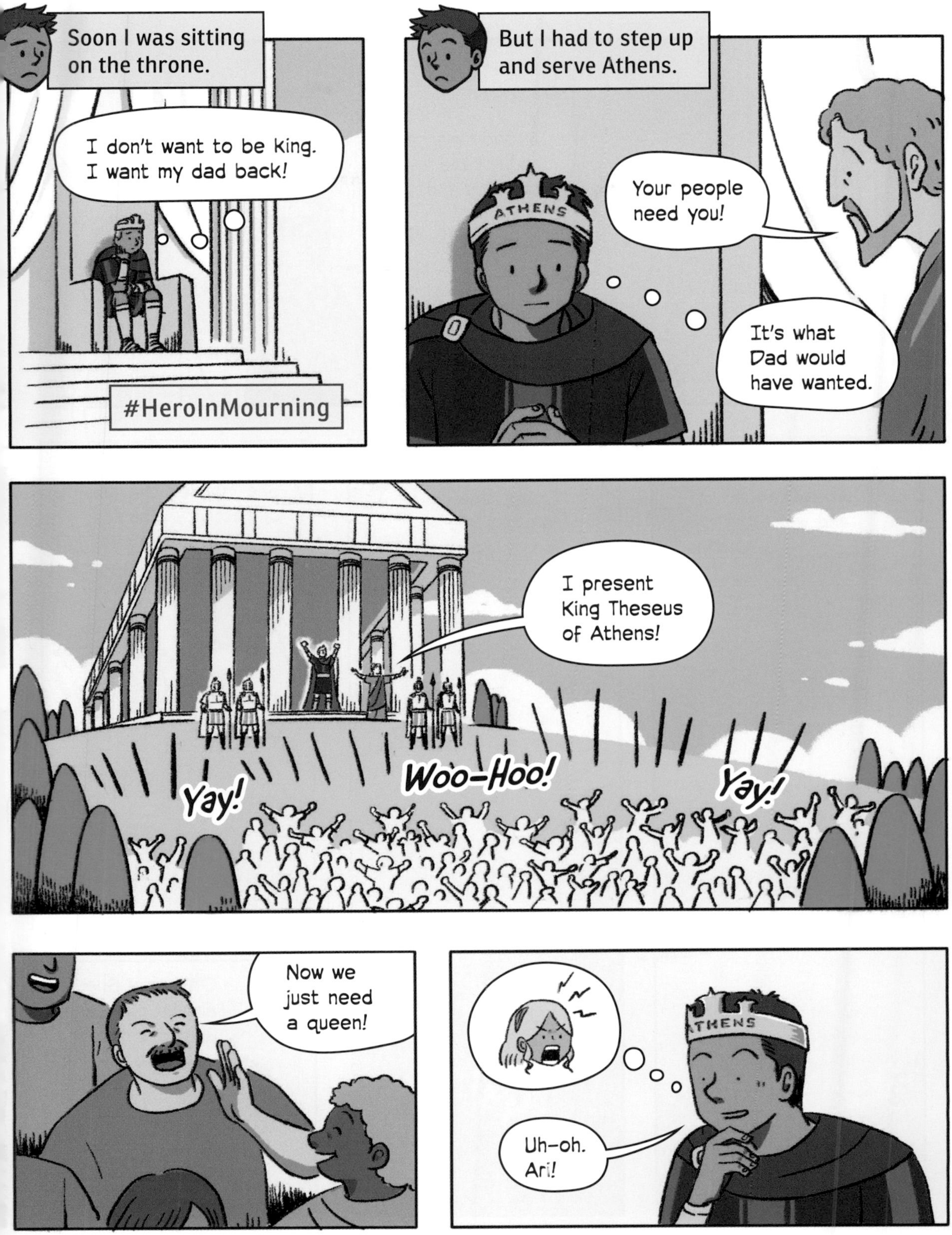
Soon I was sitting on the throne.
I don't want to be king. I want my dad back!
#HeroInMourning
But I had to step up and serve Athens.
ATHENS
Your people need you!
It's what Dad would have wanted.
I present King Theseus of Athens!
Yay!
Woo-Hoo!
Yay!
Now we just need a queen!
ATHENS
Uh-oh. Ari!

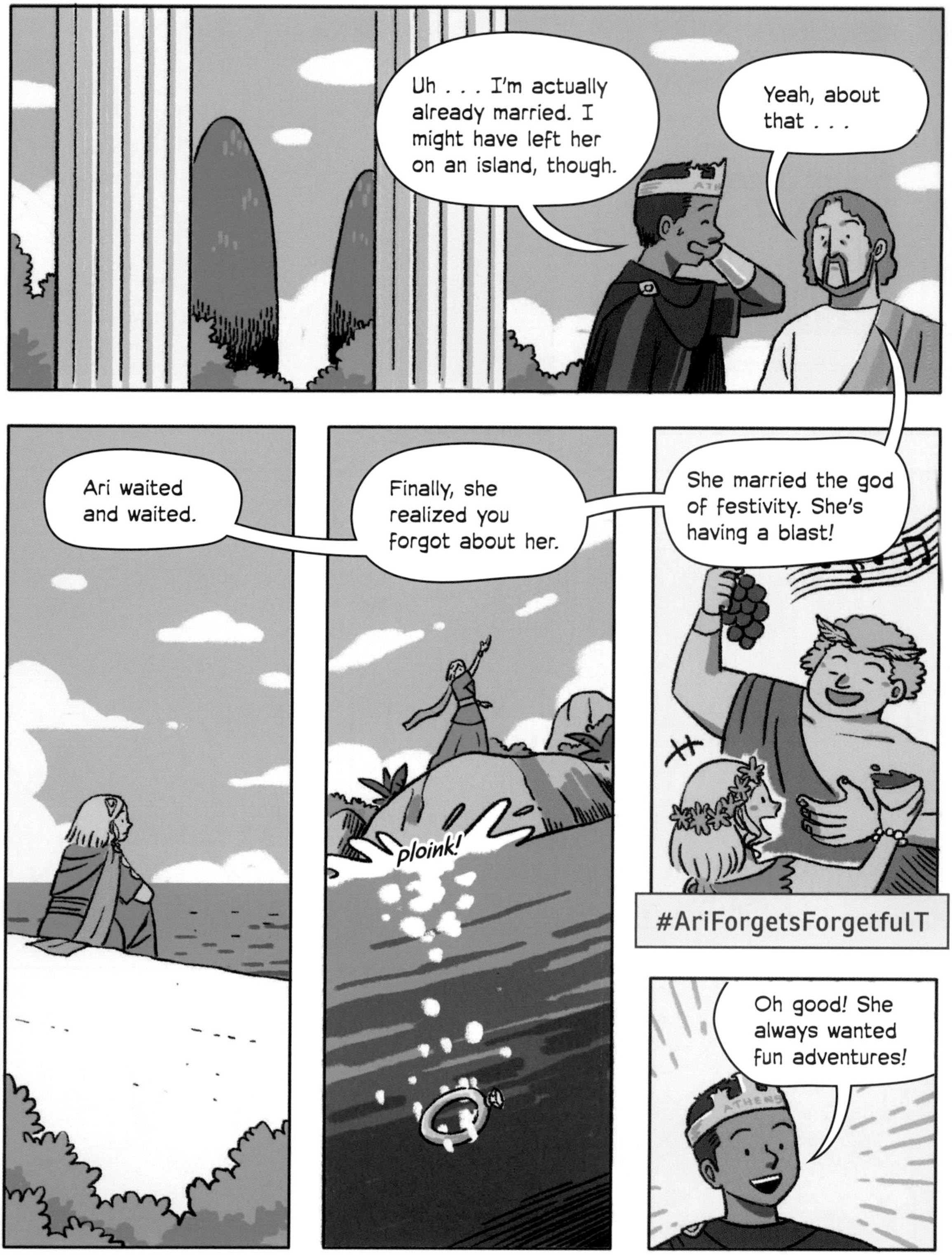
Uh . . . I'm actually already married. I might have left her on an island, though.
Yeah, about that . . .
Ari waited and waited.
Finally, she realized you forgot about her.
ploink!
She married the god of festivity. She's having a blast!
#AriForgetsForgetfulT
Oh good! She always wanted fun adventures!

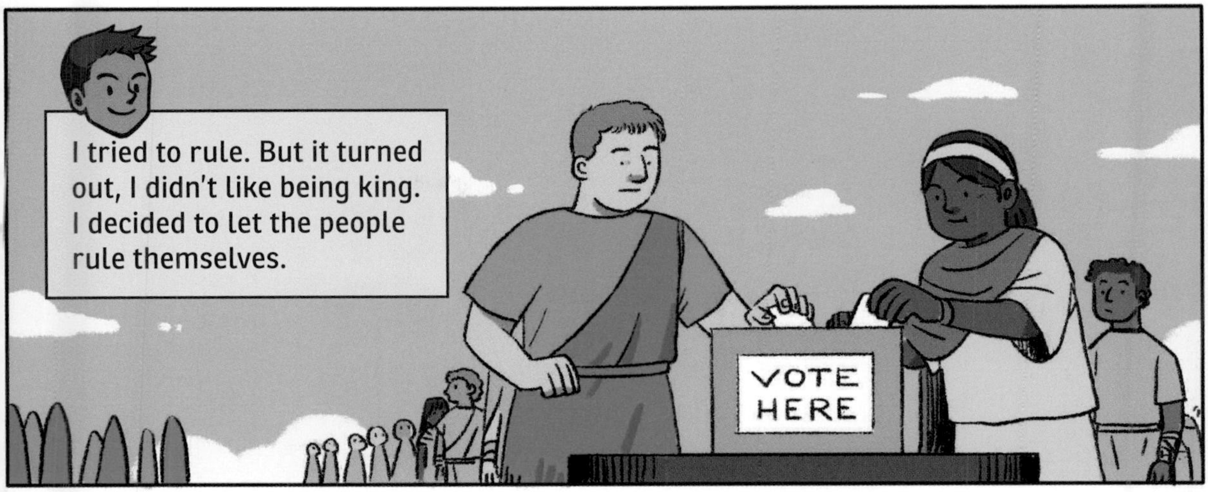
I tried to rule. But it turned out, I didn't like being king. I decided to let the people rule themselves.
VOTE HERE

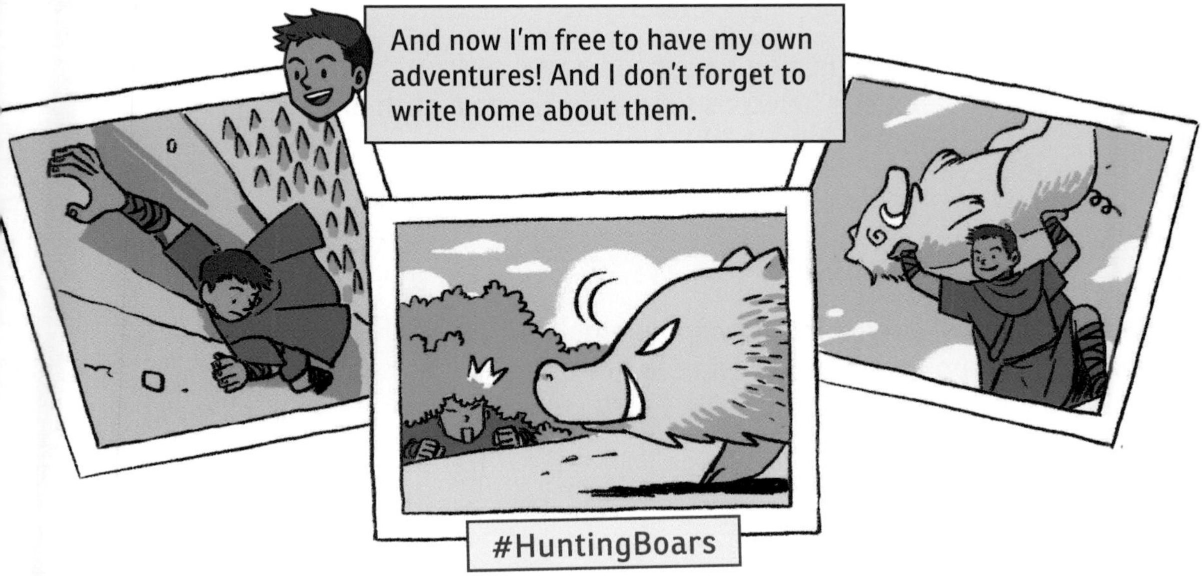
And now I'm free to have my own adventures! And I don't forget to write home about them.
#HuntingBoars

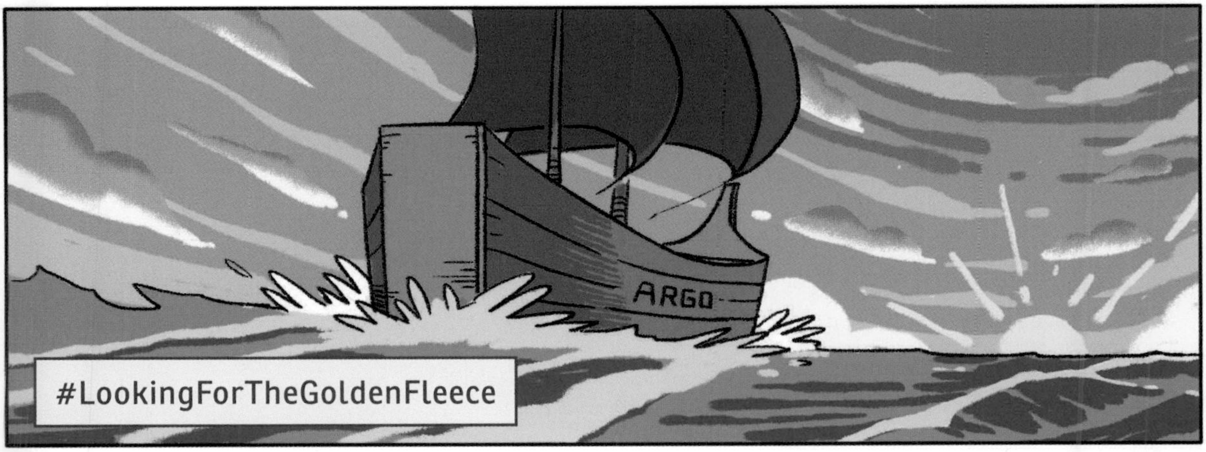
ARGO
#LookingForTheGoldenFleece

More About Theseus and the Minotaur

Theseus may have been a real person. Some believe he was a king alive in the eighth or ninth century BCE.

When Theseus arrived in Athens, the king's wife tried to poison him. She wanted her own son to be the heir to the throne.

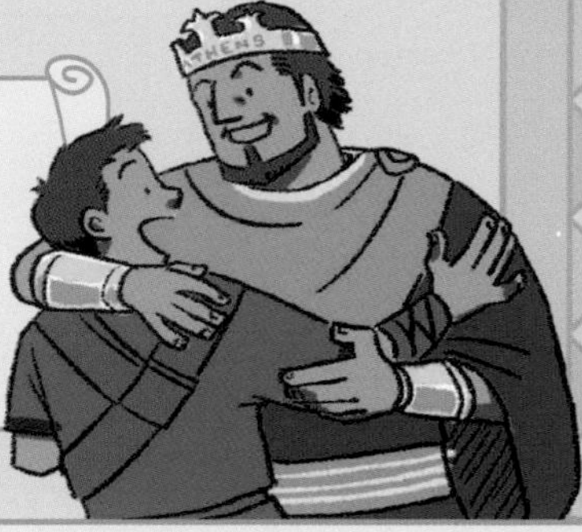
ATHENS

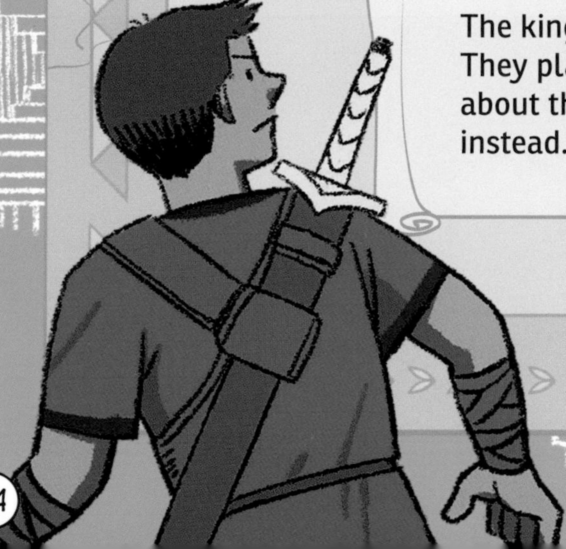

The king's nephews also tried to kill Theseus. They planned a surprise attack. Theseus heard about their plan, though, and surprised them instead.

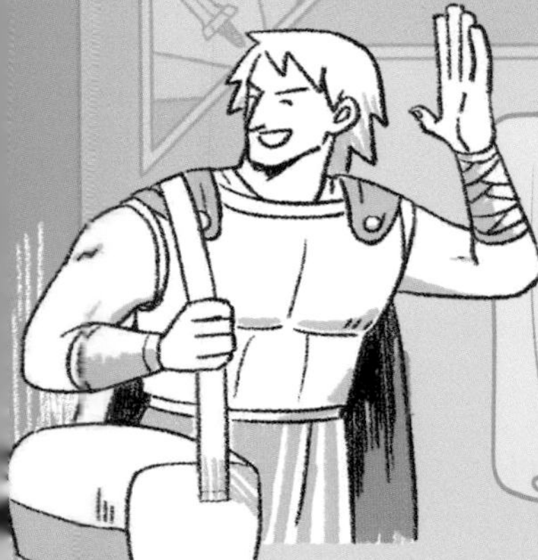

King Minos's son was named Androgeus. Different myths tell different versions of his death. Some say he was killed after competing in the Panathenaic Games. The games were like the ancient Olympics.

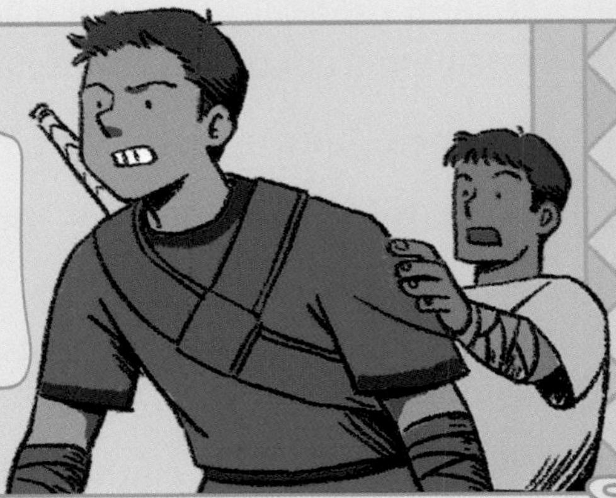

Theseus eventually married again. He wed Phaedra, another daughter of King Minos.

Theseus had a best friend named Pirithous. The two tried to rescue Persephone, daughter of the goddess Demeter, from the Underworld. They failed, and Pirithous remained in the Underworld.

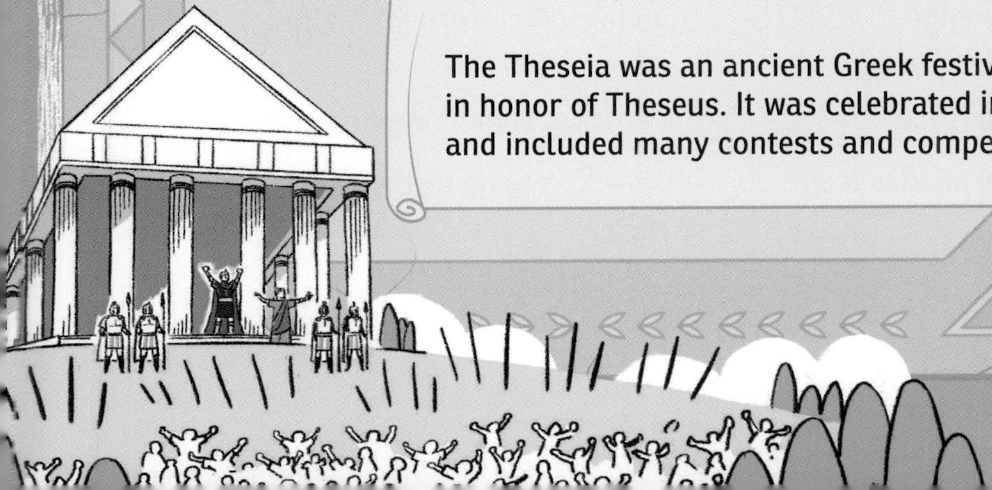

The Theseia was an ancient Greek festival held in honor of Theseus. It was celebrated in Athens and included many contests and competitions.

GLOSSARY

advantage (ad-VAN-tij)—benefit or gain

architect (AR-ki-tekt)—a person who designs and draws plans for buildings, bridges, and other construction projects

bandit (BAN-dit)—a person who lives by attacking or stealing from travelers, often as a member of a band

banned (BAND)—forbidden

festivity (fe-STIV-uh-tee)—the quality or state of being joyful and fun

heir (AIR)—someone who has been or will be left a title, property, or money

labyrinth (LAB-uh-rinth)—a maze of winding passageways that is difficult to find the way out of

Minotaur (MIN-uh-tawr)—in mythology, a monster that had the head of a bull on the body of a man; the Minotaur was confined in a labyrinth until Theseus killed it

ogre (OH-ger)—an ugly giant of fairy tales and folklore that eats people

revenge (rih-VENJ)—action taken in return for an injury or offense

sacrifice (SAK-ruh-fisse)—to offer something to a god

suspicious (suh-spish-uhs)—expressing distrust

INTERNET SITES

Britannica Kids—Greek Mythology
kids.britannica.com/kids/article/Greek-mythology/598932

Theseus and the Minotaur
greece.mrdonn.org/theseus.html

Theseus and the Minotaur: Story for Kids!
www.theoi.com/articles/theseus-and-the-minotaur-story-for-kids/

OTHER BOOKS IN THIS SERIES

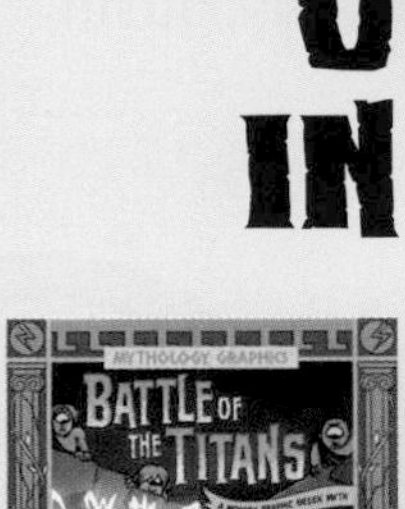
MYTHOLOGY GRAPHICS
BATTLE OF THE TITANS

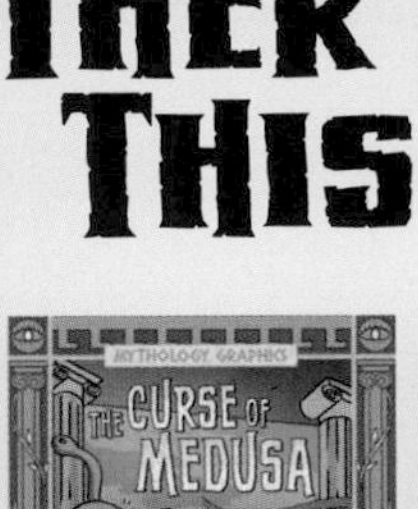
MYTHOLOGY GRAPHICS
THE CURSE OF MEDUSA

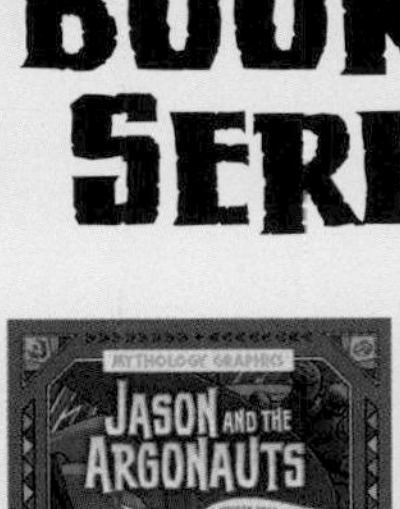
MYTHOLOGY GRAPHICS
JASON AND THE ARGONAUTS

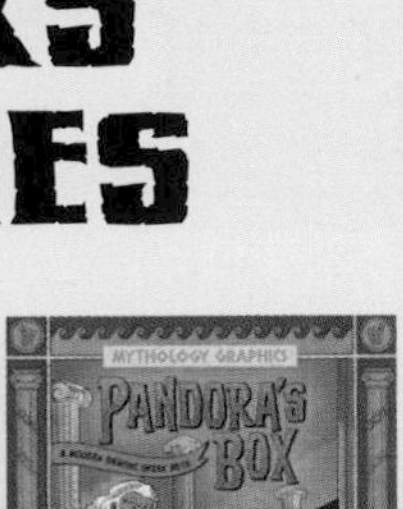
MYTHOLOGY GRAPHICS
PANDORA'S BOX

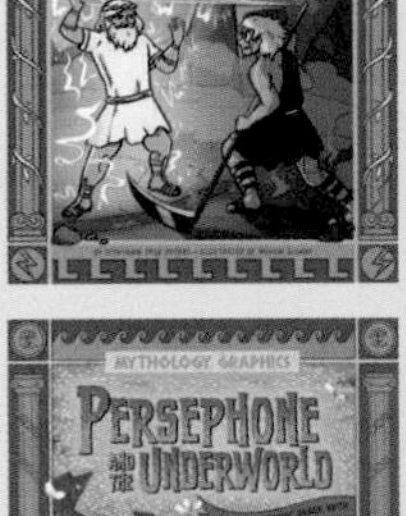
MYTHOLOGY GRAPHICS
PERSEPHONE AND THE UNDERWORLD

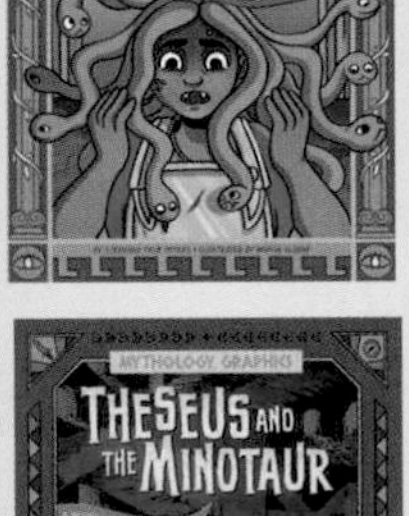
MYTHOLOGY GRAPHICS
THESEUS AND THE MINOTAUR

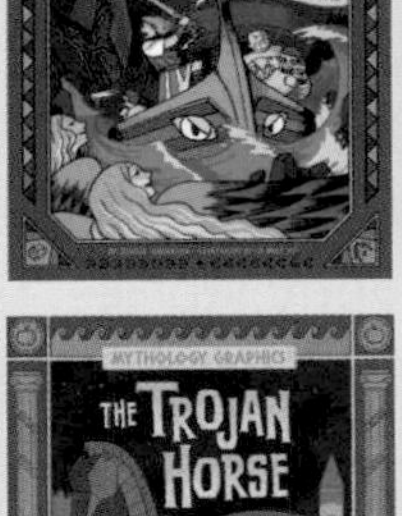
MYTHOLOGY GRAPHICS
THE TROJAN HORSE

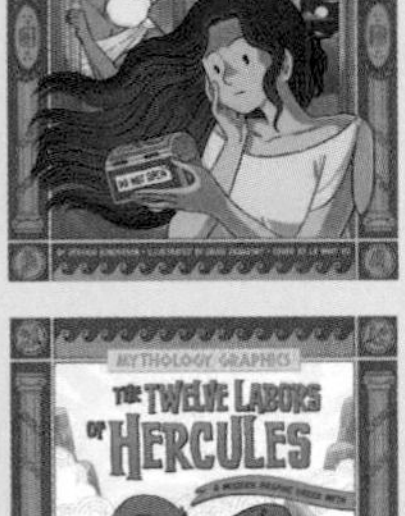
MYTHOLOGY GRAPHICS
THE TWELVE LABORS OF HERCULES

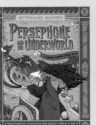

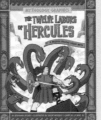

ABOUT THE CREATORS

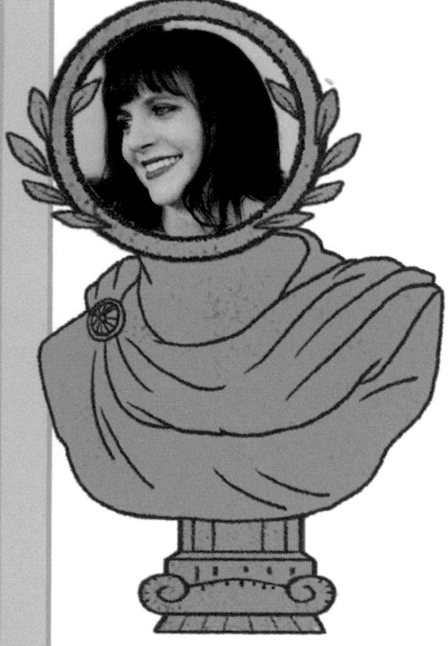

Jessica Gunderson grew up in the small town of Washburn, North Dakota. She has a bachelor's degree from the University of North Dakota and an MFA in Creative Writing from Minnesota State University, Mankato. She has written more than one hundred books for young readers. Her book *President Lincoln's Killer and the America He Left Behind* won a 2018 Eureka! Nonfiction Children's Book Silver Award. She currently lives in Madison, Wisconsin.

Le Nhat Vu was born in Nha Trang, a seaside city in Vietnam. He now works as a book illustrator in Ho Chi Minh City. He draws inspiration from fantasy, adventure, and poetic stories. During his free time, he enjoys reading Japanese comics (manga) and novels as well as watching football and movies—maybe with a cup of milk coffee.

Photo Credit: Le Nhat Vu

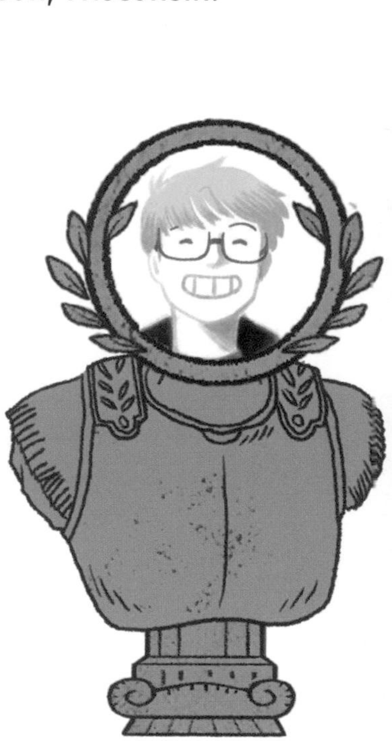